LETTING GO AND LIVING

The Story of St Columba's Hospice

YVONNE BOSTOCK

LETTING GO AND LIVING

THE STORY OF ST. COLUMBA'S HOSPICE

YVONNE BOSTOCK

Copyright © Yvonne Bostock, 1991

First published 1991 by

St Columba's Hospice
Challenger Lodge
Boswall Road
Edinburgh EH5 3RW

ISBN   0 9518143 0 3

Cover by James Hutcheson

Typesetting by David Macdonald Ltd., Edinburgh.
Printed by Billings & Sons Ltd., Worcester.

PREFACE

Stop anyone on Princes Street in Edinburgh and ask them what they know about St Columba's. They will tell you it is the Hospice down in Trinity – where people who have an incurable illness spend their last days. Many will have been there and even more will know someone who has died there. Some will tell you they have made a donation through a sponsored event, by buying something at one of the charity shops or by simply putting their spare change in a collecting tin. Others have been actively involved in fund-raising or working there as a volunteer. There are few people living in Edinburgh whose lives have not been touched in some way by St Columba's and many in Edinburgh, Scotland and further afield have taken the Hospice to their hearts. They want to know what lies behind the relaxed, homely atmosphere of the elegant Georgian house with its modern extensions and well kept grounds. How was the Hospice started and why? Who were the people responsible for it? This book has been written to answer these questions and to describe the aims, ideals and philosophy behind St Columba's.

CONTENTS

ACKNOWLEDGEMENTS

I should like to acknowledge the following people for their contribution and help:

Ann Weatherill, Dr Derek Doyle, Jeanie Simpson, David Meehan, Alastair Drysdale, Bishop Richard Holloway, Katy Cooper, Pam Rodger, Shirley Sibbald, Joan Cooper, Derek Murray, Dr Fred Benton, Dr Ian Campbell, Dr Jack Wilkinson, Dr David Strachan, Dr Gena Halliday, Dr Pru Barron, John and Barbara Simpson, Ronnie Ironside, Andrew and Sheana Monteath, Katharine Weir, Roz Hotoph, Meg McKenzie, Tom Bell, Alex Cassie, Evalyn Temple, Mark Gorman, Dr Ian Thompson, Alison Thompson, Professor John Smythe and Mary Young.

I should also like to thank Jeanie Simpson, Mary McCallum, Jane Paxton, Alison Allan and all the nurses for allowing me to be part of their team and for teaching me so much in such a short time.

As a patient, David Rennie played a special part and I remember him for that. My thanks also to John, Camilla and Jason for their encouragement and to Dr Derek White for valuable guidance and his support. For the understanding to write ' Letting Go and Living', I am grateful to my father.

I am particularly indebted, of course, to all the governors, staff, patients and volunteers – some of whom are not named here – who shared their memories, reminiscences, views and opinions with me. This is their story.

INTRODUCTION

The modern hospice movement began in Britain with the work of Dame Cicely Saunders, the founder and first medical director of St Christopher's Hospice in London. As a recently qualified social worker, Dame Cicely had cared for a young Jewish patient who was dying. Both the young man, who was a refugee from Hitler's Germany, and Dame Cicely recognised that he needed far more than the hospital could offer. He needed to belong, to give meaning to his life and to make his peace before he died.

The idea that ultimately led to the founding of St Christopher's grew out of this encounter. When he died the young man left £500 as a founding gift – as "a window in your home". He died reconciled to himself and his faith. By asking Dame Cicely for "what is in your mind and in your heart" he had said that he needed not only the skills and competence of modern medicine but also the compassion and companionship of caring.

The Hospice movement is not new. For centuries hospices have been places where the sick, aged and dying were cared for and where the poor and needy could expect to find welcoming protection. The need to look again at what these places offered arose from the emergence of modern medicine and the way in which hospitals cared for patients.

The scientific study of medicine in this century, with its emphasis on the function of the body as a machine, made possible enormous advances in curing and treating disease and illness. There were major developments in drug therapy, spare part surgery, micro-surgery and, in particular, the treatment of cancer by radiotherapy and chemotherapy. These developments, however, had their drawbacks. Hospitals became places where patients were treated as bodies rather than people. Patients found themselves stripped of their identity in an alien and often comfortless environment, surrounded by frightening equipment. Busy staff, caught up with hospital routine and procedures, had less and less time for words of comfort. Trained to deal with the case or emergency in hand, the belief was that by applying the correct and efficient, if impersonal, treatment, cure would be effected. New surgical techniques, drug treatments and other therapies enhanced the continued emphasis on cure. Medicine increasingly became a battle in which doctors were locked in combat with death, so much so that the individual patient's need for care and attention was overlooked. Death in the hospital setting and in society generally came to mean failure – doctors were seen as "having lost the battle" to save life. To many doctors and nurses, who saw their job as saving life, a dying patient represented their own failure – rather than a human being with an overwhelming need for care and compassion. As contact with dying patients was kept to a minimum, these patients were often left on their own for long periods and many faced death in loneliness and isolation.

What was happening in hospitals was a reflection of the way society dealt with death. Death became, and still is, a taboo subject – not easily talked about in company. Euphemisms were used when referring to death. Neighbours crossed the street to avoid meeting the gaze of a recently bereaved widow. The rituals of death, the careful washing and laying out of the body and the last act of loving and caring were surrendered to undertakers and funeral directors to be carried out impersonally away from the family and away from the living.

If we are honest, we can understand why so many of us run away from those nearing the end of their lives and avoid talking about death and dying. Most of us, including the doctors we so readily condemn, are frightened of death – our own death. At the least, we have some fear or awe of death. Yet the reality is that the end of life is the one certain thing we all have to face – whether it comes quickly on the golf course or after an illness that gives time to prepare.

The climate of opinion is now changing and we are beginning to recognise that both the living and the dying have to deal with death and need help to do so. Taking death from under wraps, talking about it, providing support and counselling for the dying and for the bereaved began with the work of those like Elisabeth Kubler-Ross in America and Cicely Saunders in this country and others involved in setting up hospices. Many of these pioneers were committed Christians or, at least, had a belief in God and a purpose in life. With their compassion and faith, these pioneers saw the need to find a better way of caring for the dying and had the courage to take on the task. Their work has shown that, whatever our beliefs, the care that is given in a hospice environment allows those suffering from terminal illness to live the end of their lives in their own way, free of pain and to die with dignity.

St. Columba's Hospice – Challenger Lodge and the nursing wing.

PART ONE

THE EARLY YEARS

Ann Weatherill

A CHAMPION FOR A CAUSE

ANN WEATHERILL'S DREAM

The founding of St Columba's in Edinburgh owes much to the Christian ideals and pioneering spirit that fostered the same sort of work south of the border. In the mid-sixties St Christopher's had been founded and other modern hospices were getting off the ground in England but there were none in Scotland. The Hospice movement was being talked about and there was a growing awareness of the work of Elisabeth Kubler-Ross and Cicely Saunders and their work with the dying. The climate in Scotland was right for the idea to take off as in other parts of Britain, but the idea needed to become a cause and the cause needed a champion who would nurture it until it took root. The woman who was to be that champion was a nurse with years of experience behind her and a desire to change the direction of her work. She had little idea that her personal goal in life would involve many more than just herself and that she would play a leading role in founding Scotland's first modern hospice.

In 1967, Ann Weatherill left her job at Berwick Hospital, where she had been Matron for four years and came to Edinburgh bringing hopes and dreams of working with the terminally ill. She was then in her early fifties and at the pinnacle of a successful nursing career, but total fulfilment and satisfaction with life eluded her. As a young nurse she had been moved and saddened to see terminally ill patients in hospital not always getting the time and attention they needed and relatives of dying patients leaving hospital with no-one to comfort them. Throughout her career she had nurtured a dream of working in terminal care nursing and had looked for ways of realising this ambition. She was a devout Christian and believed that, if this was the work that God intended for her, He would present the opportunity when the time was right. In 1967 she thought this time had finally come. She had the offer of a job in Australia and was all set to embark on a new life doing the work that for so long had been close to her heart. At what was almost the eleventh hour, another twist of fate presented her with the opportunity to stay and work in Scotland. Her family and friends, who were less than enthusiastic about her plans to go to the other side of the world, persuaded her to apply for the post of Matron at the Corstorphine Hospital in Edinburgh. She was offered the job and decided to take it in the hope that some other opportunity to do terminal nursing would present itself.

She threw herself into her new job but still the frustration remained. The problem, of how best to deal with terminally ill patients and the distress suffered by relatives, would not go away:

"The problem niggled away at me, especially when people were dying and I saw the relatives going down the hospital drive desolate. We were always tight on staff and there wasn't time to sit and stay with people – not as much as I would have wished."

She raised the problem with her own priest, the hospital chaplain and a number of her church friends but, while there was great sympathy, no-one could come up with any practical solutions. The turning point came when Ann was asked by Father Chancellor, Rector of Old St Paul's Church, if she would be attending a talk to be given by Cicely Saunders at the Royal Infirmary of Edinburgh. The name meant nothing to her at that time, but she went along to listen to Dr Saunders who had just opened St Christopher's Hospice for the care of the terminally ill in London. After the talk Ann met Dr Saunders and, inspired by what she had heard and aware it might be a way of realising her own hopes, accepted an invitation to spend three weeks as a volunteer helper at St Christopher's.

The experience was everything she expected. She was happy in the work among staff who could give their undivided time and attention to patients and where the atmosphere was so different from that of a normal hospital ward. There was reassurance that she was embarking on something worthwhile:

"As soon as I arrived there I could feel the peace, contentment and joy enfolding me."

Ann came back full of enthusiasm and anxious to tell everyone about St Christopher's. The description of peace and contentment was scornfully dismissed as a "typically female reaction" by one Edinburgh businessman who was interested in the practicalities of a hospice but had little understanding that supportive attitudes and ways of caring for patients could produce a very different atmosphere. At a later date, when he visited the Hospice himself, he was to eat his own words and very humbly admit that she was right – the welcoming atmosphere was evident even to a cynical hard-nosed businessman.

While Ann had the idea of a hospice for Edinburgh, she knew that it was not something she could do alone. She needed help to make it a reality. Soon after her visit to St Christopher's, Ann gathered around her a small group of friends who began to talk, think and plan for an Edinburgh hospice. Margaret Strathdee was a nurse who had been working at Corstorphine Hospital with Ann. She too had an interest in the hospice movement and followed the same course as Ann by spending a period of time working at St Christopher's. Margaret Strathdee, her husband John, and Tom Bell, who was Ann's lawyer, joined Ann Weatherill to form the core of this group. At this time Ann was living in the hospital. On her evenings off she would escape to Tom and Anne Bell's home in Murrayfield Gardens, spread her papers and plans out on the table in their big old-fashioned kitchen and work on a strategy. These were good times, with old friends dropping in, working together and enjoying companionship and hospitality.

In May 1967 Ann presented a paper to a meeting of nursing and medical staff of the Royal Infirmary. By now her enthusiasm was mounting and she was anxious to get something off the ground. At this stage the plans were modest – the idea of a separate unit had still to take shape. She was hoping for a decision to set aside a ward at Corstorphine Hospital where terminally ill patients could be nursed. The committee was enthusiastic about the idea and she went away hopeful, trusting that something would come of her proposal. The months passed with no response and no sign of action.

Despairing of ever getting anywhere with her plan, Ann went to see Bishop Carey, the Episcopal Bishop of Edinburgh. Her old friend and ally Father Brady, the Rector of St Michael's Church, accompanied her on this visit. Bishop Carey listened attentively, sat for a long time without saying a word, while she explained what she wanted to do and why it was so important. Finally she finished and he looked up, smiled and said "When we get the Hospice...". After months of talking, thinking, dreaming, planning, Ann felt that, at last, someone was listening to her and taking her seriously – the relief was enormous.

Soon there was also encouragement from other sources. With the involvement of Tom Bell, there was an ever widening group of professional and business people who saw a need for a hospice. In January 1969, Dr Saunders was invited to address a meeting in Edinburgh which was attended by well over one hundred and fifty representatives of the churches and the medical and nursing professions. Everyone there was interested and nearly a hundred of those who attended the meeting went on to Tom Bell's home to discuss plans further. What happened that evening turned out to be a real turning point and many saw the occasion as being the foundation of the Hospice.

DEREK DOYLE JOINS THE GROUP

Early in 1969 Dr Derek Doyle took up a part-time post at the Corstorphine Hospital. He was a committed and practical Christian and had spent ten years working as a medical missionary in Africa. Having returned to Scotland with his wife and young family, he had embarked on a career in general practice. He was well known locally, a highly regarded GP, happily settled in his new work and looking forward to life continuing that way for some time. Working with Ann Weatherill at Corstorphine Hospital was to change all this. After joining the staff there he soon discovered that, as a Matron and as a person, Ann Weatherill was a woman with considerable leadership skills:

"She was a real old fashioned Matron and ran the place with a handful of staff. She had a sense that she really knew what was wanted for patients. She knew how to keep staff together and draw out loyalty. Everyone called her 'Mother' in the old fashioned tradition. It really was quite an experience to be part of that. She was a very firm disciplinarian – dependable. You knew you could follow her."

When Ann Weatherill asked him one day, almost in passing in the middle of a busy round, what he thought of a hospice for Edinburgh, his experience and instincts told him that this was a project to get involved in. He was no more knowledgeable about the practicalities than Ann Weatherill but he had years of working as a missionary and knew that, if you believe wholeheartedly in the value of something, it could be made to happen. Derek Doyle joined the small group which was to be the driving force behind the setting up of the Hospice. He added his voice to those involved in raising funds and addressing groups. Like Ann Weatherill, he was a good speaker and was able to gather support with his ideas about the kind of medical care that a hospice could offer.

By now the small group had grown to include Ann, Derek, Father Earnest Brady, Maurice Heggie, Dr Morris

Mancor and Dr Earnest Cormack. Through church connections, Women's Guilds and Rotary Groups, Ann Weatherill travelled further and further afield – as far north as Wick and Thurso and south as Dumfries. For the most part, she was successful in persuading people that a hospice, where terminally ill patients could receive good nursing care and their families the support to see them through the distress of bereavement, was much needed. Many wanted the hospice, not only for what it could do for the people of Edinburgh, but for the changes it could bring to the care of the terminally ill throughout Scotland. The concept of a hospice as a place was beginning to take root, and the whole philosophy of a way of caring for the dying – much more than just the bricks and mortar – was beginning to be understood.

Despite the growing interest and enthusiasm, there were difficulties. Not everyone who heard Ann Weatherill or Derek Doyle was won over and there was considerable opposition. Some were unable to listen attentively to detailed discussions about death and dying and these talks often aroused as much apprehension as compassion. Ann Weatherill recognised this and accepted that she could not convince everyone:

"There were those who didn't want to know, the fear was just too much for them. When people don't want to know about death, it is because they themselves are frightened of their own death."

They also came up against the problem that many doctors were sceptical. The very fact that such a group had come into being was seen by many in the medical profession as a criticism of hospital care. It took time and patience to get the message over that this was far more important than simply pointing the finger of blame and that dying patients needed more than hospitals were able to offer. They needed prompt attention, relief of pain and discomfort and the support of staff who were not afraid of death and who had time to sit with them. Most importantly, they needed to be where the truth that cure was not possible could be accepted. Relatives needed to be able to come and go, to understand the illness and to be able to share the truth with their loved one. What was proposed would benefit doctors, nurses and patients. It would free the patient and all involved in caring for him or her from the stress of keeping up a pretence. Once the truth was acknowledged, it was only a short step to accepting that life is too precious to be ruled by hospital routine. In the last weeks or days, patients should be given every care and comfort and, where possible, have their wishes met. Acute hospital wards were too busy and their staff numbers too few to meet these needs. Perhaps understandably, they concentrated on patients where there was a prospect of cure or at least a return to the family. A hospice, designed to be more like a home and staffed with appropriately trained doctors and nurses, could give a very different service to that of a general hospital. What seems to make good sense now was new and different then and the antipathy was difficult to break through. They were treading a fine line. On the one hand it was necessary to point out the inadequacies of hospital care to make their case, provoking antagonism, yet they needed the support of medical colleagues. Added to that, the apparent whims of well-meaning people carried little weight in a profession which made decisions on the basis of scientific evidence. There was little such evidence to point to and not much to show that hospices worked.

These were difficult times but enthusiasm and belief in what they were doing kept the small group going. With faith and conviction, they resisted the cynicism of others. If anything, opposition made Ann Weatherill more determined. Talking with a small group from her church one evening early in January 1968, a young American, who thought she was "a silly old woman" and that the whole thing was too impossible for words, tossed her a shilling and said she would never do it. That night she taped the shilling to a mirror as a constant reminder of her determination to establish a hospice in Edinburgh. Had he lived, the young man would have enjoyed knowing he had played some small part in the whole challenge. Sadly, he died eighteen months before the Hospice was opened.

In January 1969 the informal committee became a working committee and, in June, Lord Birsay agreed to be its first chairman. Lord Birsay suggested naming the hospice after St Columba – the Irish monk who brought Christianity to Iona and made missionary journeys to the Highlands. He also suggested that the Bishop of Edinburgh, Dr Kenneth Carey, because of his support and encouragement, be asked if he would be a patron along with the then Lady Primrose (later to become the Countess of Rosebery). The committee also took the decision to seek charitable status. The Hospice was another step closer to realisation. John Simpson, who joined the committee in 1969 and became Honorary Secretary, was responsible for drawing up the Articles of Association and floating the company which was formed in 1971.

In September 1970 Ann Weatherill was awarded the Lady Louis Mountbatten travel fellowship which allowed her to visit all the English hospices and gain further experience of hospice work. St Columba's was beginning to take shape and as she, Derek Doyle and the rest of the committee continued to promote it to ministers, priests and doctors, the idea was becoming more firmly established in the minds of some of the most influential members of the community.

CHALLENGER LODGE – A HOME FOR THE HOSPICE

THE SEARCH

Despite his grand title, Lord Birsay was an approachable man and held in great affection and esteem. He and his wife knew something of suffering in the world. Lady Birsay, a doctor, was among the first to go into Belsen in 1945 at the end of the war. Lord Birsay had been a successful QC and was chairman of the Land Court. John Simpson describes him as an "entree to anything and the friend of everyone". Under his chairmanship the committee gained confidence and direction and grew to sixteen in 1970. Meeting in John Simpson's office in Alva Street, it included representatives from the legal, medical and clerical professions. The members at this time were Lord Birsay, Ann Weatherill, Georgina Adams, Margaret Strathdee, Brigadier Allan, Tom Bell, Reverend Peter Clark, Reverend Donald Cole, Dr Derek Doyle, J Gregson, Maurice Heggie, Dr Morris Mancor, John Simpson, John Strathdee, Professor L Gordon Whitby and Dr James Williamson. Of these Lord Birsay, Ann Weatherill, Tom Bell Maurice Heggie, John Simpson, John and Margaret Strathdee and Dr James Williamson signed the Memoradum and became the first Board of Directors.

They were a formidable group with influence and clout and were respected members of the community. They were also a relatively privileged group – all leading busy lives. Why did they get involved with a hospice for Edinburgh? No doubt motives varied. It was a good cause and perhaps, if friends asked, it was impossible to refuse. Some simply felt that power and privilege also carried responsibility. The one thing they all had in common was a belief that the Hospice could do much good, although not everyone had the sense of involvement that came from a deep religious commitment. The idea of a hospice and its ability to fulfil such basic human needs was reason enough to get involved. For several it would seem that the motivation was more down-to-earth than heavenly:

"Everyone helped spread the Gospel, but you did it for purely practical reasons. We wanted a place where people who were dying of cancer or some other disease could be treated well and their relatives looked after. It was about care not cure. I didn't feel that the Almighty wanted us to do the task, but I was sure He wouldn't mind."

By now the committee had decided that they wanted a purpose built hospice and Lord Birsay and John Simpson had a meeting with Dr Henry Raeburn, Chief Administrative Medical Officer of the South East of Scotland Regional Hospital Board (later to become Lothian Health Board), in the hope of getting help with a suitable plot of land. The contact looked promising. The Health Board had land at Southfield and an architect was commissioned to sketch out rough plans and estimate costings. He came up with a figure of £1,000,000. The sum was an impossible one for spare-time fund raisers. The plan was abandoned and the small group pressed on exploring other avenues.

Properties that sounded ideal came on the market but nothing materialised and set-backs and disappointments continued. The committee dug themselves in for what was to be five years of fund-raising and property-hunting. The money was trickling in but funds were still very small in relation to the size of the task. By now they had a few tins in shops and pubs but asking people to give to something, which looked to many like a pipe-dream, was an up-hill struggle. Yet, once people understood what it was all about, they came up with fund-raising ideas that fired others with enthusiasm and inspired people to give. The husband of one of the staff nurses at Beechmount hospital was the chef at a local hotel. He started a 'swear penny' pile – the 'bluer' the language, the more staff had to contribute to a good cause. Eventually the pile of pennies reached well over £100. It was a great encouragement and demonstrated that larger sums could be raised.

There was now a core fund as a result of the people of Edinburgh digging into their pockets. The coffee mornings, jumble sales, sponsored silences and carol-singing all continued with friends, relatives and children joining in. By this time Evalyn and Arthur Temple were involved and Elizabeth and Pat Wimbush. They and their children helped with the fund-raising and were later to play an important part when the Hospice building was purchased. For those caught up in the enthusiasm of St Columba's, it was a way of life before it was a building or was even known by that name.

Contributions in the form of bric-a-brac, books, cushions, pictures and furniture were coming in. Despite the slow progress and the difficulties, there was no giving up. Everything was either carefully stock-piled for use later in the Hospice or sold to raise funds.

Meanwhile, the search for suitable premises continued. Early in 1975, Miss Enid Dickie of the Cripple Aid Society contacted Barbara Simpson, the wife of the secretary John Simpson, and Barbara Dale-Green, one of the Governors, and informed them that a house owned by the Society was about to come up for sale. The description of the house, its size and location sounded promising and they lost no time in following up the 'tip-off'. They inspected it, saw its possibilities and took Derek Doyle and Ann Weatherill to look at the property, then a children's home and appropriately named Challenger Lodge. First impressions were encouraging. It had grounds for extension and the right atmosphere. On a clear day the views across the Forth would be superb and the house, which was a listed Playfair building, could be renovated to meet the needs of a modern hospice. To others the drawbacks were all too obvious. Challenger Lodge could be seen as run down and in a terrible state of disrepair – a sad and neglected, albeit

Georgian, pile. In their enthusiasm and all too aware of the disappointments and set-backs so far, Derek Doyle and Ann Weatherill saw only the potential and what Challenger Lodge could be. As far as they were concerned, it was ideal for their purpose.

SECURING THE PURCHASE

The rest of the committee were equally enthusiastic about Challenger Lodge. There was only one stumbling block and a large one at that – how would they pay for it? This was February 1975. The property was up for sale at £145,000. The committee negotiated the figure down to £125,00, with the Cripple Aid Society agreeing to an initial payment of £50,000. However, with only £40,000 in the bank at that time, they could not even cover the deposit. But the offer was too good to turn down and, if they let it go, they would be faced with the daunting task of starting the search again. Believing that the rest of the money would be raised, it was decided to go ahead with the purchase. Some of the committee saw the decision as an act of faith. Others took the practical view that, once Challenger Lodge was purchased, the rest of the money could be raised by tapping the right sources. Both proved right – £25,000 was paid over and, by the end of April, the shortfall on the deposit had been made up by a grant from the Gannochy Trust.

It had taken five years to find Challenger Lodge but the Hospice now had a home, albeit in need of much work. Edinburgh folk could see that these Hospice people meant business. A party was held to celebrate and guests asked to bring a gift that could be sold to raise money. A huge debt of £75,000 was still outstanding. It was clear that, while the jumble sales had set the ball rolling, some very large sums were needed to clear the balance. It was time to recruit someone who could deal with this next stage of fund-raising and Barbara Simpson was asked to take on this task.

Barbara set about approaching the charitable trusts. As well as having worked as a hospital almoner, she was then a Director of the Queen Elizabeth Fund for the Disabled – the ideal background for the job in hand. She had been drawn into fund-raising for the group through her husband and through Ann Weatherill:

"I was inspired by her absolute dedication. I so admired what she was trying to do that I got involved – we played bridge to raise money, had coffee mornings and parties but in those days it was very 'pie-in-the-sky' and it was difficult to raise money for something that did not exist".

Once Challenger Lodge was purchased and the Hospice was no longer 'pie-in-the-sky', the visible bricks and mortar inspired confidence. By now Derek Doyle was deeply involved in formulating plans for the care of patients and a clear philosophy was emerging. They were setting their standards high. St Columba's was to be about the best in quality of nursing and medical care, management and all aspects of providing for patients' everyday comforts and needs. The chairman of the Mary Kinross Trust, who visited Challenger Lodge and heard first-hand about the plans for the Hospice, responded with a grant of £30,000. Most of the large trusts gave between £5,000 and £10,000. With money being donated in such large sums, the committee's faith had not been misplaced. Whether through God, good fortune, good management or a combination of all three, the Hospice was a going concern.

By September of the same year, 1975, Barbara Simpson and her team had raised £78,000. It was an amazing achievement. The purchase of Challenger Lodge was completed. The whole transaction was settled without borrowing from a bank or building society. The committee could now get down to planning the renovations for the opening of the Hospice.

GETTING READY

In January 1976 Kathleen (Katy) Cooper took up the post of Administrative Director. She came to Edinburgh from London where she had been working for the cosmetics company Yardley. She had also been an officer in the WRAC. Her task was to get Challenger Lodge organised from the administrative side. Although she had no experience of hospice work, her admiration for those who said, "It can't be done but it will be done", inspired her to take up the challenge. Derek Doyle by this time was acting volunteer Medical Adviser but Katy Cooper was the first paid employee. As well as being responsible for supplies, household needs and setting up administrative procedures, her job was to co-ordinate the plans for the opening and to ensure that everything went according to schedule. With her background and army experience, Katy Cooper was a stickler for efficiency and high standards. She felt very strongly that the Hospice should never fail to live up to what it claimed:

"A voluntary unit that sets out to be highly professional has no excuses – it has to provide the best care for everyone all of the time. That's the basis on which you ask for money and there's no failing to live up to those standards."

The time had also come to appoint staff who would be responsible for raising and managing funds. Shirley Sibbald joined as assistant to Katy Cooper in the same year. Later, after the Hospice opened in 1978, Roz Callender was appointed as Appeals Officer. While Barbara Simpson took on the Trusts, Shirley Sibbald began to take an interest in looking after the money raised and setting up accounting procedures. In September 1977 she was given full-time responsibility for this when she was appointed Finance Officer.

Buying the house was the beginning of a long process of getting it ready for use as a hospice. It was some time before contractors could move in to start work and there was still plenty for volunteers to do. Initial renovations were confined to Challenger Lodge itself. Two main rooms on the ground floor, with their views of the sea, were to be the wards and accommodate fifteen beds. Cleaning, painting and sorting out years of accumulated junk began in earnest. Alex Cassie, who was a night-porter at Corstorphine Hospital, started work on the garden with help from others including boys from Edinburgh Academy. Fruit and vegetables were sold to raise money. Ann Weatherill and her friends began making the "comforts" – the Shetland shawls, night-dresses and draw sheets that would make life easier for patients. Ann was still working at Corstorphine Hospital which meant that patients there were used as guinea pigs to try out her ideas and they also benefited from these little luxuries. They in turn left hospital to tell friends and neighbours about the plans for the hospice.

The furnishings were organised. Much of these had been donated. Even curtains and carpets had come from well-wishers. No apologies were made for using second-hand. It was good housekeeping and kept much needed funds for essential patient care. More importantly, rather than a show-piece, everyone wanted Challenger Lodge to be welcoming – a place where patients felt comfortable and at ease in a setting that was not too different from their own homes.

While building work went on, the children of volunteers and workers had the run of the grounds. Shirley Sibbald and Dee Goldie had older daughters who looked after the younger ones. When the summer was over Margaret Strathdee carried on with a creche for the children of patients, staff and volunteers. The primary aim was to support families and it was to prove a godsend for young couples with small children where one partner was dying. It gave them the opportunity to spend much needed time together. While no-one thought of it as pioneering, this practical response to the needs of young families was one of the early work-place nurseries. It meant the Hospice kept their well-trained staff and many young people, who had contact with the Hospice through the creche,

Katy Cooper

Joan Cooper being presented with the proceeds of a children's jumble sale.
(Photo courtesy of The Evening News, Edinburgh)

went on to be volunteers or follow careers in nursing or medicine.

Ann Weatherill was never in any doubt that a small chapel would be at the heart of the Hospice and a separate fund was set up to provide for it. To set the ball rolling, a group of friends decided they would save three-penny pieces. Jars of three-penny bits were accumulated until 1971 when decimilisation simplified the coinage and half-pennies were collected instead. Even so, when the going got difficult, the committee looked to the Chapel fund to augment the down-payment on Challenger Lodge. Ann resisted this pressure insisting that the fund be kept and that the Chapel was an essential part of the Hospice. When Challenger Lodge was purchased, one of the rooms in the East wing was designated for this purpose and a start was made on collecting the necessary furnishings.

It was inevitable and understandable that with all the activity at Challenger Lodge, as it was converted into what was then an unknown institution, there was mounting anxiety among local residents. What would it mean for them? Would they be living in the constant shadow of death and funeral corteges? What would happen to property values with death on the doorstep? As with any situation when people are only half informed, rumours began to fly. It was decided that the only way to deal with these anxieties was to hold a meeting and tell those living in the neighbourhood what was happening and what the Hospice aimed to do. The local people listened. This was all new to them but it was not long before the Hospice was accepted as part of the community and very soon many of the local residents were offering their help and rolling up their sleeves with the rest.

MEDICAL AND NURSING STAFF

By 1977 Derek Doyle's involvement with the Hospice spanned eight years. When he had joined Ann Weatherill in 1969 it had

Dee Goldie being presented with a cheque for a sponsored cycle from
Land's End to John O'Groats.

(Photo courtesy of The Evening News, Edinburgh)

Dr Derek Doyle and Jeanie Simpson.

not been with a view to leaving General Practice to work in the Hospice. However, as plans proceeded and the time came for the Board of Governors to appoint a Medical Director, there was no-one better qualified. Although he was appointed Honorary Medical Director early in 1977, it was not until September that he gave up his practice and took on the job full-time.

With Derek Doyle formally in post, the next key appointment was that of Matron. The post was advertised in the late summer. Joan Cooper was living and working in Bournemouth at the time after working overseas for many years. In late 1977 she was contemplating taking a job in Oman. She applied for the post at St Columba's but time passed and it seemed that she was not in the running. Her passage to Oman was booked and her bags packed when she heard she had been short-listed for the Edinburgh job. Her background was ideal. She had considerable experience of working in intensive care and of having set up and administered units in hospitals in Oman. She had also nursed her husband before he died. Her instincts told her to delay the flight out to Oman. She was good at getting things started and this was what St Columba's needed – someone to get it up and running. She went for the interview, was offered and accepted the job.

Shortly after Joan Cooper took up her post, Dee Goldie was appointed as Home Care Sister. She had first met Derek Doyle in 1955 and had subsequently worked with him for a time in the seventies. Along with Derek Doyle, her job was to get the Home Care Service established. It had always been envisaged that Hospice care would include a support system to help GPs and relatives look after patients in their own homes. Advice and assistance on pain and symptom control would be given by Hospice staff but the patient would remain in the care of his or her own doctor. Only in the event of being admitted to the Hospice would the patient become the responsibility of the doctors there. The demand for the service took off immediately and, within a few months of Dee Goldie's appointment, a second Home Care Sister was appointed early in 1978. To complete the senior appointments Derek Murray, a Baptist minister, took up the post of part-time Chaplain.

Staff and auxiliary nurses for the Hospice itself were then interviewed – all of them new to working in an environment geared to the care of the terminally ill. The week before the Hospice was due to open an orientation course was held for the staff. Through a series of lectures and discussions involving Derek Doyle, Joan Cooper, Derek Murray and Katy Cooper, staff were introduced to the philosophy of the Hospice. While nurses were taught in their general training how to deal with dying patients, at that time there were no specific courses on Terminal Care. These lectures were the beginning of a more formal educational programme that was to become an important part of the work. Within a short time a Nurse Tutor was in post and district and hospital nurses were invited to the Hospice to learn about Terminal Care as it was practised there.

During this time approaches were also made to Lothian Health Board for practical assistance in running the Hospice and in October 1977 St Columba's was recognised as a Nursing Home. This meant that all necessary pharmaceutical and other supplies and services could be obtained at basic cost and access to laboratories and the ambulance service was assured. Approaches were also made to the Board, in the period prior to opening, for further funding to help meet running costs but this was not yet forthcoming.

PREPARING FOR PATIENTS AND FAMILIES

Once medical and senior staff appointments were made, there were all the practicalities of catering for patients and their families to discuss. How would staff handle the situation on the ward when a patient died? How could they best provide the last and final care of laying out? The ideal arrangement was a special area, a sanctuary, but until the further extensions were built this care had to be given within the existing building. Provision had to be made also for a place where relatives had peace and quiet to be alone with their loved one. Those who had worked with the terminally ill knew that these last moments together were important for relatives. If the illness was difficult and painful, the family needed the relief of knowing that death brought peace. For many it was an important part of the acceptance of death and allowed them to move on to, and through, the grieving process.

Care and concern for the patient and relatives was to be total – until the patient finally left St Columba's. The same care was to go into handing on the responsibility. Local funeral directors were invited to a meeting at which the senior staff spelled out this total care. Arrangements would be handled sensitively for the sake of the patient who had died, the relatives and the remaining patients.

The care of the patient was never considered in isolation from the needs of the patient's family. Within the Hospice, the Sister or Staff nurse would maintain contact and provide as much support as possible. The Home Care Sisters would provide on-going support for patients' families at home. They knew how important it was to be sensitive to these needs – to listen to a wife pouring out anger and frustration because her husband was 'leaving her', or simply to offer a comforting shoulder to cry on. But what about afterwards and providing on-going support through what was often a long and difficult grieving process? A number of volunteers, some of whom had themselves been widowed and had worked through their own grief and bereavement, formed a support group. They had an ability to listen and an understanding of what people go through in losing someone close. Widows, widowers, sons or daughters could be put in touch with them if they wanted help. The importance of small gestures was recognised and it was decided that a card – a note of remembrance – would be sent to the relative on the first anniversary of the death of a patient.

The Chapel

Presentation of the sampler quilt by the Thistle Quilters, 1986.
(Photo courtesy of The Evening News, Edinburgh)

THE CHAPEL

With the Half-penny Fund, the small room in the East wing was converted into a place of peace and rest for private prayer, a quiet time, meditation or reflection. Like much of the decorating and refurbishing elsewhere, work on the Chapel was undertaken by volunteers. Arthur Temple, along with his family, was responsible for the painting and repairs. The decoration of the original chapel was simple but beautiful – fitting for a place where those of every church affiliation could worship. It was enhanced by a colour scheme designed to create a peaceful atmosphere. The walls were painted grey contrasted with white woodwork and a purple ceiling. A charcoal grey carpet and grey-blue curtains complemented the scheme.

The artist, Sylvia Benert, designed a motif – depicting the sign of the cross and the dove with a half circle of light behind denoting the resurrection – to be the symbol of St Columba's. She sketched it onto a large canvas which was then made up into a tapestry. Worked in subtle shades of blue, grey and white, the tapestry was woven with Ann Weatherill's help. Although originally designed as a rug, it was decided to hang it on the wall where it would provide a backdrop for the Holy Table.

The Holy Table itself and the minister's chair were made by an ecclesiastical carver, Colin Almack, known as the "Beaver Man of Thirsk". The story behind the name goes back to his days as an apprentice with Robert Thompson. Ann Weatherill had known Robert Thompson as a village carpenter, when he had used the expression "poor as a church mouse" so often that he had adopted the sign of a mouse as his trademark. Known as "The Mouse Man of Kilburn", he had insisted that his young apprentices choose their own sign. Colin Almack chose to be known by the sign of a beaver. The table is clearly inscribed to the right; and the tiny carved beaver, sitting cheekily on the arm of the chair, fits well with the almost light-hearted atmosphere in the Chapel.

Well-wishers gave or made other furnishings such as the kneelers and chairs. The Thistle Quilters of Edinburgh donated a beautiful sampler quilt made up of twenty four squares. Each one is different and represents a particular biblical reference. The squares were pieced by members of the Quilters Quandary, a group within the Ann Arbor, Michigan branch of the Embroiderer's Guild, and sent to Edinburgh to be quilted individually and then assembled by members of Thistle Quilters. The quilt was hung on the back wall facing the minister and creating a backdrop for the congregation. A priest at Dalry and his elderly mother donated the silver anointing box. An old couple gave a cruet set to celebrate their golden wedding. The poetess, Marian Lockhead, wrote a poem which was illuminated by a nurse at Corstorphine Hospital. The Blue Lodge of London sent a painting of the Head of Christ done by Rosenkrantz. It was hung on the wall of the chapel and, no matter where one stands in the chapel, the eyes of Christ are on you. St Columba's Church in Dundee sent a statue of St Columba which was placed in the credence alcove above the altar. A cushion was covered with the remnant of a piece of coronation brocade for a bishop's chair – a handsome but uncomfortable piece of furniture. The remnant, a beautiful blue with a crown design in gold, was found in an Edinburgh junk shop. Furnishings, upholstery and a set of vestments were all completed in time for the opening of the Hospice. The Chapel was not to be dedicated to one particular denomination of the church and, in keeping with this, it had everything that any minister or priest could want.

THE FOUNDING 'MOTHER'

It was as much a tribute to the people of Edinburgh who had given generously from their limited pensions and wages that the big trusts came in with large-scale funding for the Hospice. The circle of people and institutions now involved had grown since the early days and the Hospice owed its existence to them all. Yet there was no doubt that Ann Weatherill's vision had been the prime motivating force. In recognition of this and for all her work there were to be honours. In 1978 she was Edinburgh's 'Citizen of the Year'. But prior to this in September 1977, three months before the Hospice was scheduled to open, Ann Weatherill was formally asked if she would accept the title of Founder. Her dream, that had begun so long ago and to which she had devoted the past ten years of her life, was about to come true and it was an honour that she was pleased to accept.

Some thought it was a sad irony that Ann Weatherill herself was never to have a nursing role at St Columba's – the cherished dream with which she had embarked on the whole mission. She had followed her star and it had taken her beyond her own ambitions. She had, in fact, done more than care for the dying herself. She had been instrumental in making it possible for many more to be cared for than she could ever have done single-handedly and she had helped provide opportunities for others to take on and continue the work of caring for the terminally ill. Just as Derek Doyle said she had 'mothered' her nurses, so too she had nurtured the Hospice. Now it had life and a momentum of its own.

THE OPENING ACT . . . OF FAITH

Katy Cooper kept a watchful eye on developments as she set the wheels in motion for the Hospice to move into action. Renovations and building works which had begun in 1976 ran into problems that knocked the schedule off course. 1976 came and went and the work continued well into 1977. Time was passing, impatience beginning to mount and questions were being asked – "All this talk! When are you going to open?".

There probably never was an ideal time for the Hospice to open its doors. At some stage it was a case of 'taking the plunge'. Money came in but went out as quickly. The Hospice had been scheduled to open by the end of 1977. The question that faced the Board of Governors when they met on September 22nd 1977, was whether they could make that deadline. The Hospice was ready but, with only sufficient funds in the bank to cover salaries for two months, it would be a gamble or an act of faith. A vote round the table was taken and the decision was unanimous. The Hospice would open on December 6th – on schedule.

December 5th dawned cold but bright. The staff, volunteers, friends and well-wishers gathered at Wardie Parish Church for a dedication and thanksgiving service. Jean Holloway, the wife of the Rector of Old St Paul's Church, had written a hymn for St Columba's which was sung then for the first time. It was a moving service, marking the end of one phase of the Hospice and the beginning of another. It had begun with a small band of dedicated people who had worked with commitment and determination. In the congregation were founders, helpers, neighbours and staff. They knew they were involved in something that had a strength and purpose of its own – greater than any one individual involved with it – and they were right. This small unit, with space for only fifteen patients, was to touch the lives and hearts and minds of many – in ways that they themselves were, as yet, unaware.

THE YEARS OF DISCOVERY

APPEALING IDEAS

Once the first patient was admitted to the Hospice and the teaching began, visitors started to flood in from all over the world. St Columba's was the first modern hospice in Scotland. Everyone was enormously proud of belonging to it and this enthusiasm was communicated to people in the community. There was great interest. Everything that was happening there was new and people wanted to know about it.

Lothian Health Board were interested but they had been wary. Here was a voluntary group looking for money. What were their aims and who would benefit from this new sort of nursing home? Was it to be a place for the privileged few? In October 1977 the Health Board had responded to an approach from the Hospice by agreeing to the provision of essential services but the question of a further grant had been temporarily shelved. When the Hospice was opened, the Board decided that the only way to resolve the issue was to go and look at the place and find the answers to these questions for themselves. The addresses of the patients very quickly cleared up the misunderstandings – there were people from Leith and Pilton as well as Trinity and Silverknowes. In 1978 Lothian Health Board approved a grant of £100,000. After 1979 a formal contractual arrangement was agreed and the Board provided substantial annual funding in recognition of the number of patients treated there who would otherwise be in hospital.

Recognising the importance of caring for patients at home, in 1978 the National Society for Cancer Relief gave a grant of £25,000 and subsequently decided to fund the Macmillan Home Care Service. This kind of funding and the grants from other charitable trusts provided a basis of much needed financial security. Yet nothing could be taken for granted and not all funding arrangements were written in tablets of stone. In 1984, as a way of stimulating home care development in other areas, the National Society for Cancer Relief decided to support new services for their first three years only and phased out its contributions to St Columba's. There was still a great need to keep the money coming in.

Hospice staff very quickly learned that talking to people was the best way of getting help from the community. With their encouragement, support groups grew up in and outside the city – in Fife and as far afield as Dumfriesshire, which raised money in any number of ways. As early as 1974 volunteers had set up a Trading Group so that small items, such as pens, diaries and cards, could be bought and sold at speaking engagements. As the need for more substantial funding became apparent, the group very quickly became more ambitious in their aims and set about other projects. They compiled their own publications. The first big money spinner was "Dial a Dodge" a telephone book with useful recipes and household hints. The publication was so successful that the group was able to persuade Harrods to stock it. This led to other ideas. Barbara Simpson had culinary skills which she set about using for the benefit of the Hospice. She produced "A Briefcase of Good Cooking" – a collection of menus and recipes from famous restaurants in and around Edinburgh. The restaurants benefited from the chance to advertise while, at the same time, doing a good turn for St Columba's. More ideas followed. Barbara Simpson invited her friends to lunch parties asking them to bring their favourite dishes. Calling themselves the "Peppermill Group", they produced the "Mill of Menus" – a cookery book that covered everything from recipes for thrifty tripe to venison in red wine. The Trading Group led eventually to the opening in 1978 of the "Gem and

Jar" a small shop which was the brainchild of Ian and Penny Kinnear. It was to be an independent enterprise for the sale of preserves, needlework and small articles of jewellery. Penny Kinnear and others slaved away in their kitchens producing dozens of pots of jam and marmalade. Sales were so successful that the shop raised £10,000 in its first year and continued in subsequent years to make a substantial contribution to Hospice funds. Later, in 1987 and 1989, the same enterprising spirit led to another two shops being opened – "The Wardrobe" in Stockbridge and "The Doo'cot" in Leith.

To Roz Callender, the Appeals Officer, it was clear that money came from all sections of the community – from the well-off raising money at their drawing room parties to the miners selling bric-a-brac in their club halls. Her job was to find as many ways as possible to keep the funds coming in. There were bazaars, jumble sales, fashion shows, sponsored "slimmings" and "grow a giant sunflower" competitions for schools. As the Hospice took off, more ideas were needed and Roz Callender went to the Queen Elizabeth Fund for the Disabled to learn about how they handled fund-raising. It was here that she got the idea for the Charlotte Square Festival which was first held in 1979 and, every alternate year since, has proved a great attraction with its marquees, stalls and entertainment of all kinds.

Nineteen eighty one was the year of the first Wits' dinner. At £17.50 a ticket, this elegant social event, held at the Assembly Hall, was for those who were prepared to pay for a good meal and a good evening's entertainment. The after-dinner speakers were to compete for the Wits' Trophy by raising as many laughs as they could. Women for the event were in short supply but, determined to prove that there were members of the fairer sex equally as funny as men, Roz Callender arranged for the American actress Elaine Stritch to fly up from London for the occasion. She would, Roz hoped, not only steal the show with her wise-cracks but dazzle the gathering with her glamour. On the day of the dinner, Roz

Roz Callender being presented with a cheque by children
from Bellevue Road, 1980.

Lord MacKay with Diana Moran (the "Green Goddess")
at the Wits' dinner, 1988.

went to collect her special guest from the airport. Slightly in awe of the star she was meeting, Roz scanned the faces of the Shuttle passengers but no-one emerged who remotely resembled the larger than life TV personality. As the crowds dwindled, only one person remained – a very ordinary, slightly dowdy, middle-aged lady wearing a plastic rain hat. "Perhaps she had missed the plane", Roz thought. Then the possible truth dawned on her. "This wasn't ... no it couldn't be ... She could hardly mistake Elaine Stritch, or could she?" She tentatively greeted the woman in the rain hat, only to discover that this was indeed the person she was waiting for. With her heart sinking and thinking the whole evening was going to be a disaster, she took her to the hotel and left wondering what had possessed her to do such a crazy thing! It was the nature of the job – some gambles paid off, others did not. She returned to the hotel to collect her guest. What happened at the dinner was a transformation that finally allowed Roz Callender to breathe a sigh of relief. The Elaine Stritch of show business emerged from the shell into which she had only temporarily (thank goodness) withdrawn. She appeared in a slinky tight-fitting evening dress and stole the show with her showbiz glitz. The gamble had paid off but despite the glamour and despite being very funny, she lost the war of words to Sir William Fraser, the then Permanent Under Secretary of State at the Scottish Office.

Personalities of all kinds have played their part in helping St Columba's over the years. Among them Roz Callender particularly remembers Jim Ede, a well-known art historian, who came to Edinburgh after a remarkable life and who not only gave works of art to the Hospice for sale but also contributed ideas. Jim Ede had been Curator of the Royal Academy and was famous for having gifted his house in Kettles Yard in Cambridge to the University. He was a great patron of the arts and artists and believed that people should learn about the beauty of nature. His house was filled with objects that created shapes and shades of light and grey. He gave it to the university as an art gallery. A highly religious man, he and his wife came to Edinburgh late in life, moved into a small house and adopted a very simple life-style. They took the Hospice to their hearts, supporting it with gifts from their collections which could be sold to raise money. Jim Ede was also a man full of ideas – many of which he passed on to Roz Callender. In 1977, a few weeks before the seventh of July (7.7.77), he suggested a radio appeal be launched to raise sums of money from £7 to £777. It was ideas like these which captured the imagination of the public. Now that the Hospice had patients and relatives who had experienced for themselves what the Hospice offered, people understood the importance of keeping it going.

Meanwhile, there was talk of the Hospice being a happy place. To many this seemed to be going too far – all these patients simply waiting to die! There were stories of people going to visit and being quite taken aback that there was a cheery atmosphere and patients moving around and not all bed-bound. There were also cases of patients going home from the Hospice, often for quite long periods. They went in for short periods to have difficult symptoms controlled. Some spent very little time as in-patients but were looked after by nurses visiting them at home. Patients who once thought of St Columba's as a death sentence were finding that the Hospice offered new hope – not of miracle cures but of restored dignity and a better quality of life in the time that was left. Later, when the Day Hospice opened, there were activities of all kinds. Somehow, everyone assumed that the atmosphere would be gloomy and sad, but from the beginning there were plenty of good times and parties when everyone enjoyed themselves. Christmas-time had seen doctors serving Christmas dinner to patients and staff and birthdays and anniversaries had been celebrated. Then in 1982, all set to leave St Columba's, marry and begin a new life in England, Roz Callender and her husband-to-be decided that the Hospice chapel was the place for the ceremony. It was the first wedding to be held at the

Gatehouse of Fleet Support Group – Flappers Ball, 1986.

Staff Nurse Jackie Quinn receiving a cheque from relatives of a patient.
(Photo courtesy of The Evening News, Edinburgh)

Matron and nurses with a sponsored walker.
(Photo courtesy of The Evening News, Edinburgh)

Trinity Academy children taking part in a schools' promotion.

Hospice and, while there were to be others, everyone remembers it as a very happy occasion. Patients and staff were all involved in the celebrations. There was wedding cake and a buttonhole for everyone and all the excitement and noise of any reception when the couple left in their car – cans and old boots rattling behind them.

Pam Rodger took over the task of keeping the money coming in - encouraging the efforts of work-mates, schoolchildren and clubs of all kinds. Over the next few years covenants increased and donations came in from churches, relatives of patients and support groups. The annual Flag Day and House-to-House collections made substantial sums of money but there could be no let-up in what was to be a never-ending task.

The latter part of the nineteen eighties saw a growth in promotional activities with local and national companies involved in sponsored events. In 1985, Duddingston Golf Club successfully hosted the first Pro-Am golf tournament which from then on became an annual feature of the golfing calendar. Another first that year was an auction held in their sale rooms by Phillips Auctioneers. There were two hundred and fifty lots, many of which were donated anonymously. In the following year, Ferranti sponsored the Scottish Ensemble New Year Gala and Alexander's sponsored a Bowls Trophy Tournament. There was also a special presentation of Andrew Lloyd Webber's 'Requiem' at the Usher Hall. Individuals contributed with their talents. Scottish actor Tom Fleming, who had done radio appeals since 1978, presented the first highly successful television appeal in 1981 and continued to support the Hospice as their media appeals spokesman. In June 1986 the first Art exhibition was held. This was organised by the "Art Friends of St Columba's Hospice" committee. A total of forty-five artists exhibited and sold their work. Christmas cards became a source of income as more people looked for ways to give and Colin Baxter, particularly famous for his landscape photography, gave the Hospice sole rights to one of his Christmas cards.

A legacy leaflet was produced in 1987 and made available through two hundred legal firms in and around Edinburgh to clients wishing to leave money to the Hospice. Company giving through matching employees' donations took off in the late eighties but in a limited way. Levi-Strauss in Livingston was the first company to match employees' donations, raised by running raffles and dances. From within companies there was also some interest in payroll giving which suited some people but not others. Pam Rodger felt that the best ways of giving in the work-place were those that also benefited the people involved:

"It would be great to get all the employees at Scottish Gas to contribute but we have six or seven active groups at Scottish Gas who support us and have fun doing things – so they get something out of it as well as giving. We've got another group in a department where there are a lot of young people who have to deal with the public – it's a very stressful job. They had a manageress who wanted to get some fun into the office. Every year they have raised hundreds of pounds for us but that manageress has said it has been a two-way process – it brought the group together. So she felt we had benefited them as much as they had us"

ORGANISING THE HELPERS

As far as the day-to-day managing of the Hospice was concerned, Evalyn Temple, who was one of the early group of volunteers, took over as Housekeeper and was responsible for the efficient running of the domestic arrangements. Regular maintenance, cooking and cleaning services were provided by paid employees. Whatever the job, the contribution it made to looking after patients was always recognised. Cleaners were as essential to the Hospice as the doctors. This still left much of the daily routine work of the Hospice to be carried out by volunteers and it soon became apparent that the quality of service was as dependent on them as on the staff. Good management and co-ordination of the work of the volunteers was essential and Sheana Monteath and Joyce Will took this job on board. Despite the need for able-bodied men for the heavier tasks and garden work (a need that remains), the vast majority of volunteers were women. Sheana Monteath organised her army of helpers in an orderly way. Everyone who wanted to work for the Hospice was interviewed to assess their skills and allocated to appropriate teams. People had their own reasons for volunteering. They knew someone who had died at St Columba's or they had had an unhappy experience of someone dying in hospital. One volunteer had read about what the Hospice hoped to do and she knew, from the experience of her father's death in hospital, how terminal illness could isolate people. She felt that her father had been "very much the patient" and the family had been excluded. Volunteers were often motivated by their own need and it was important to find the right job where they could make a contribution. If a volunteer herself had been recently bereaved, she might be encouraged to help with fund-raising rather than to do work which would bring her into contact with patients and relatives. Meeting in the Murray room, named after the first owner of Challenger Lodge, teams of women gathered to sort out duties. In no time there were five hundred volunteers doing a variety of jobs. They collected tins, addressed envelopes, looked after the gardens, attended to plants and flowers in the wards, served as tea-ladies and receptionists and provided a sitter service for carers looking after terminally ill relatives at home.

Initially, Derek Doyle was the only staff doctor. Later he was joined, on a part-time basis, by Dr Gena Halliday and assisted by two volunteers – Dr. Pru Barron and Dr. Brian Carmichael, both of whom also subsequently joined the staff as part-time doctors. Pru Barron also took over responsibility for co-ordinating the bereavement counselling service, which the social worker June Campbell had organised as early as 1978. Over the years Pru Barron developed a close working relationship with CRUSE, the national bereavement counselling service, and this was formalised in 1983. CRUSE was then asked to take on this work, train volunteers and bring in some of their own team to help families of patients.

BUILDING DEVELOPMENTS

Even before the Hospice was opened, work on extending St Columba's was on the drawing board. It began in 1980 and was completed later that year with the new wing being fully functional by 1981. The extension doubled the number of beds from fifteen to thirty. The move from the main house meant that patients lost the sea view. There were other losses. More staff were needed for the increase in patients. The Hospice was suddenly much bigger, more spread out and the new arrangement was less "homely". But there were also many gains. The extension transformed St Columba's into a modern purpose-built Hospice that was much better equipped to function as a specialist clinical unit. Already the Hospice was making a reputation for itself as a leader in the field of Palliative Medicine, as the new specialty was now being called. The new unit was a measure of the Hospice's success in achieving its aims of providing both the best in medical treatment and compassionate caring. The growth in numbers brought enthusiastic young nurses keen to learn and work with terminally ill patients. Patients now had views of the grounds and gardens and the activity at the front of the house. The greater number of patients brought more families into the Hospice and links with the community expanded rapidly.

The refurbishment of Challenger Lodge also provided for new facilities. A physiotherapy room was added where the physiotherapist was able to give treatment that was previously unavailable. The chapel was moved to the original North Ward, making it more accessible to patients. The West Ward was released for use as a Day Hospice and an Occupational Therapist appointed. This service was provided for patients,

Lord Birsay with Patrick Ross-Smith and his design for
the sanctuary window, 1980.

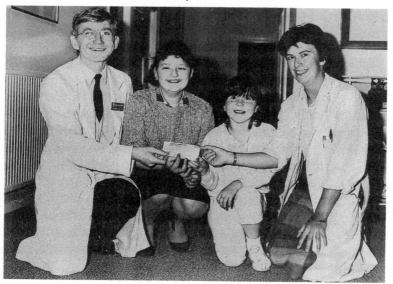

Dr Fred Benton with a medical student receiving a cheque.

Patients in the Day Hospice.

Ann Weatherill and Lady Birsay holding a shawl that Ann gave to
Lady Birsay at the formal opening of the Birsay Hall, 1985.

who were being looked after by Home Care Sisters, as well as patients in the Hospice who wanted to take part in the activities. Bringing some patients into the Hospice also lessened the load on the Home Care Sisters and meant that patients could get out of their homes and into a different environment. Coaching in crafts was provided, there were ideas for new hobbies and entertainment was offered. As confidence grew so did the sense of adventure. Outings were planned. There were excursions to exhibitions, music, poetry and dance. Through all of this, as much as the care on the wards, St Columba's became known as a place for the reaffirmation of love and living rather than a specialist centre for pain-free dying.

The refurbishment and extension also led to a demand for more helpers. Drivers were needed to ferry patients to and from the Day Hospice. Volunteers were needed to run the Murray Room which was now used as a common room for staff and volunteers. Part of the new wing had been made into a large sitting room, the Iona Room, for patients' families and friends. Volunteers were needed to provide tea and refreshments there.

There was a much needed sanctuary in the new wing. It was a peaceful room, removed from all the activity of the Hospice, where bereaved relatives could spend time in privacy with a loved one. The room was simply furnished. A stained glass window, designed by an art student Patrick Ross-Smith, incorporated the dove and cross motif of St Columba's. It looked out onto a small garden of remembrance – a quiet corner of the Hospice grounds which in the summer months is a blaze of colour.

EDUCATIONAL WORK

As the reputation of the Hospice grew so too did the demand for courses, conferences and seminars. People came from Scotland, the U.K. and overseas to attend them and it soon became apparent that existing premises were inadequate. It was decided that a purpose-built teaching wing, designed to meet this growing demand, was needed. Work began on the new educational facilities in 1984.

In 1983 Dr Fred Benton joined the staff, replacing Dr Gena Halliday who left to take charge of the Fife Macmillan Service. Dr Benton came from the Western General Hospital where he was Senior Registrar in the Department of Radiation Oncology before being appointed Consultant in Palliative Medicine at St Columba's. Both he and Derek Doyle were given Honorary Consultantships in Palliative Medicine by Lothian Health Board and membership of the clinical teaching staff of Edinburgh University. Teaching commitments expanded greatly. Courses were run for under-graduate and post-graduate doctors, nurses, midwives and health visitors. The Pastoral Studies Unit provided opportunities for future ministers and priests to study the pastoral care of the dying and to learn from the many different disciplines integrated into the care team. There was input to courses for the paramedicals – psychologists, occupational therapists and physiotherapists. Being at the forefront of the Hospice movement brought honours and responsibilities. Derek Doyle was appointed Chairman of the Association for Palliative Medicine of Great Britain and Ireland, later, Vice-Chairman of the European Association for Palliative Medicine; Katy Cooper was asked to be Chairman of the Association of Hospice Administrators; and Jeanie Simpson, who by 1983 had taken over from Dee Goldie as Nursing Director, became Chairman of the Hospice Nurse Managers Forum of the Royal College of Nurses and a member of the Executive of the European Association of Palliative Care.

When the new educational wing was completed in 1985, Lady Birsay formally opened the main lecture hall named after her late husband. The ceremony was attended by representatives from the civic, medical and professional areas of the city.

In the fourteen years of the Hospice's history, much was achieved on the educational front and St Columba's is now recognised world wide as an educational centre that has made a valuable contribution to helping students of all disciplines involved in Palliative Care. In 1987 Palliative Medicine became a full specialty with its own rigorous training programme. Early in 1989, St Columba's became the first independent hospice in Britain to have a Senior Registrar training programme approved by the Joint Committee on Higher Medical Training of the Royal College of Physicians, London, marking the development of Palliative Medicine as a newly recognised specialty and St Columba's as a leader in professional training. Students visited the Hospice from home and abroad and its staff were invited to teach and lecture in cities throughout Europe, North America, Africa and Australia. The world's only professional scientific journal devoted to palliative care – "Palliative Medicine" – established its editorial office at St Columba's with Derek Doyle as its Editor-in-Chief. No less than six books and nearly fifty papers and chapters for books were produced by the professional staff. Many of these publications became standard texts in Britain, South Africa, Singapore, Germany and Japan.

THE HOME CARE SERVICE

As soon as the Hospice opened the Home Care Service was also under way. It was financed largely by the Macmillan Fund of the National Society for Cancer Relief and very quickly proved to be invaluable. At the same time a 24-hour answering service was established and became an important element of the service, assisting patients who could not be admitted. It was described as a "survival kit" by one relative looking after her husband at home, "knowing that willing, skilful and caring help was available simply by dialling a number". Professionals used the service for consultation and the Hospice began to benefit from the assistance given by consultants as

The Queen's visit 1987 –
Her Majesty the Queen with Lord Grieve, Ann Weatherill and Tom Bell.

The Duchess of Kent with a patient and his small daughter, 1989.
(Photo courtesy of The Evening News, Edinburgh)

good working relationships with the medical profession were established. The service provided a link between in-patient care at the Hospice, the Day Hospice and the General Practitioners and District Nurses in the community. They explained to patients, families and friends the nature and course of the disease and the steps that could be taken to alleviate the symptoms. They put families in touch with other social and health services, helped the family to prepare for bereavement and supported them through that difficult time.

TEN YEARS ON

The first ten years of the Hospice tell a story of what can be achieved when people believe in something and the ability of a good cause to cut across class and social barriers. The people who contributed are too numerous to mention. Friends of the Hospice know them well. Members of the Board of Governors gave of their time, expertise and knowledge. Medical men, who believed there was a better way of caring for the dying, brought the work of the Hospice to the notice of their colleagues. Men with business ideas and know-how saw building projects through to completion. Lawyers and accountants gave sound legal and financial advice, all of which kept the Hospice on the right path. Women with practical skills as well as enterprising ideas, including Ann Weatherill who carried on sewing and fund-raising for her beloved Hospice, put them to good use. From 1976 the medical, nursing and pastoral care of patients was guided by a Professional Advisory Committee made up of hospital specialists, GPs, nurses, clergy and others. Drawing on considerable expertise, they provided back-up, support and advice to the staff and made an invaluable contribution to the development of the professional work of the Hospice. The Hospice was fortunate in having much-loved and esteemed Chairmen in Lord Birsay and later Lord Grieve; and the staunch support of its President, the Countess of Rosebery. In their turn, all of those who have contributed to the work of the Hospice tell of the pleasure and satisfaction they gained from being involved in something so worthwhile.

There were many important visitors over the years interested to know about, support and encourage the work. The Duchess of Kent, herself personally interested in the Hospice movement, visited in 1989. The greatest honour of all was that of the Queen's visit to mark the special anniversary year in 1987. It was a warm summer's day in June. Staff, patients and volunteers waited, anxious that all should go well. When she arrived it was the Queen herself who put everyone at ease, chatting informally and happily with the patients in the Day Hospice, helping to blow out birthday candles and talking to young nurses, governors, staff and volunteers.

The Queen's visit highlighted the celebration of ten years of the Hospice. St Columba's was now a well-established institution in Edinburgh. Through its reputation, stories of local people and the teaching, it had become famous throughout Scotland and the world. Like a magnet it attracted people who came to learn about death and dying but who left having learned about life and living.

PART TWO

THE HOSPICE TO-DAY

A SAFE PLACE

THE NEED FOR A HOSPICE

Derek Doyle, Medical Director and one of the original group who founded the Hospice, has been largely responsible for the development of the way in which terminal care is practised at St Columba's. In 1987 he was created an OBE for his part in it all. His belief in the value of his work and that of his colleagues is profound and utterly unshakeable but his reputation for charisma sometimes alarms him and those who know that he is as down-to-earth as most. It is lunch-time but, despite the smell of good food wafting from the kitchen, he settles for low-fat yoghurt and fruit, explaining that he is watching his waistline. He talks enthusiastically about his work, illustrating it with stories of people, what they have said and how they have behaved.

So why did he get drawn into the Hospice movement and St Columba's? Derek Doyle sees his own involvement as stemming from the changes that were happening in medicine as well as his own desire to bring true compassion back into caring for patients. The development of hospice care came about as a result of what he describes as an imbalance in medicine, particularly in the field of cancer care:

"There was disenchantment about the way cancer care was going – the preoccupation with chemotherapy. We had so many blood tests that doctors had forgotten blood came from people. The Hospice movement was very strong in Britain – but that's largely because we have a different tradition of medicine here to the USA and Canada. We've never been totally preoccupied with high tech and, because of the NHS, we've never been totally money oriented. British doctors have never regarded the body as a mechanism which, provided you can get the best technology, you'd be able to repair – which is the US, and to some extent Canadian, concept. The Hospice Movement is strong in both of these countries, but in Canada it developed very professionally whilst in the USA it is mainly run by volunteers with continuing scepticism and suspicion by professionals. While there are nearly two thousand 'Hospice Services' in the US, there are only eighteen in-patient units."

Did the fact that Britain was rather different from the States in having a system of General Practice play a part in this?

"General Practice in this country changed in the late fifties. This resistance to moving too far in the direction of high tech medicine was given impetus with the development then of the Royal College of General Practitioners and the new contract for doctors in the nineteen-sixties, which meant that more doctors would go into General Practice instead of hospitals. General Practice began to attract people of a high academic standard who were looking at a whole spectrum of psychological, social and sexual problems and General Practice became less of a sorting office for hospitals. At the same time as these changes were happening, there was a return of missionaries, Christian doctors and nurses, who still had something of the old missionary spirit, who got involved in setting up hospices."

What it led to was a resurgence of what can only be described as an 'holistic' approach to caring, but 'holistic' is not used in the glib Californian 'alternative cult' sense. Far from being a new idea, it goes back a long way:

"This is far more than terminal care, care of the dying, pain control, restoration of dignity – it is actually saying to the medical profession, 'It is safe to get back to the age old truth that you can get alongside your patient, to talk honestly, to cry with a patient, to say, I don't have an answer, but I still have myself, and to prescribe yourself as a fellow human being'. It is safe to talk to a person about their pain and about their spirituality. As well as asking if their bowels have moved, it is quite right and essential and safe to talk about how they are getting on with their nearest and dearest but we've got away from that. We have fragmented care with doctors dealing with bodies, social workers with social and emotional problems. It is truly a rediscovery of what our forefathers knew instinctively – you don't look after one bit of the body, you look after that person."

It is clear from this that Hospice care means far more than relief of symptoms or palliation. It means a deep respect for each patient's emotional, social and spiritual needs as well as those of the relatives, which is why the chaplain is an indispensable member of the care team. While it requires that doctors and nurses bring their personal qualities of ordinary human beings to the care of patients, they do not have to be saints. At the same time, technical expertise is no less important:

"What we are saying to our colleagues is, it is safe to sit on a bed, hold a person for a minute and say, 'I don't know what I can do, what would you like me to do?' That may sound a very simple thing to say but it is unusual for doctors who normally take a medical history and tell a patient what they need. But we are not saying, 'leave your high tech, your scientific medicine'. We are saying, 'let's marry some of the old truths with our modern scientific medicine'. I can't look after my patients here without CT scanners, ultra-sound and so on."

Fred Benton also sees a need to communicate that there is this balance in the work of St Columba's and that it is a medical unit first and foremost. The "everyone is so good here" attitude that prevails irritates him and, he believes, does the Hospice no good. Like others, he sees staff who provide hospice care in a hospital setting as doing a more difficult job than those in the Hospice. Having worked in a Radiotherapy unit, he knows how busy and hectic it is and that it is not an easy environment in which to look after patients. The priority is to get the treatment right. He sees his job at the Hospice as being a lot easier than in a busy high tech unit. The idea that the Hospice somehow exists in opposition to such units and that high tech equals bad medicine does not reflect the reality. St Columba's is well integrated with the NHS and there is a great deal of interchange – Hospice doctors working in close co-operation with hospital medical and nursing staff. Nor, in Fred Benton's experience, are those who work at St Columba's in any way different to the staff found in a general hospital. They may have particular skills that equip them well for the job but they are as human as their colleagues – they have good days and bad days. They make mistakes. Relatives are sometimes disappointed that a patient is not being looked after in the way that they would wish or that not enough is being done to relieve pain. Sometimes there are misunderstandings. It is also recognised that while hospice care is important for all terminally ill patients, it would be unrealistic to think that the Hospice itself is the right place for everyone. Patients suffering from some conditions, such as chronic bronchitis, need very specialised medical care. Others may want to be in the middle of the hubbub of a general ward if the staff can give them the attention they need.

THE IMPORTANCE OF TEACHING

It was never intended that the Hospice should become a sanctuary for the terminally ill, isolated from the rest of the community. This could have been an easy trap to fall into. The Hospice would have become then a special institution – a ghetto – separating off the dying from the living. Entrenched attitudes to death and dying, and the idea that the Hospice would relieve others of work that held no attraction for them, had to be resisted. Nor did Derek Doyle set out to establish the Hospice as the only place where terminally ill patients could receive good care from people who were the "experts" in palliative medicine. When he took on the job of Medical

Director, he was convinced that what happened inside had to be taken beyond the walls of St Columba's. While totally dedicated to the work within the Hospice and the needs of patients and relatives, he believed St Columba's could not exist in isolation from Edinburgh's great medical and nursing traditions and institutions and had much to gain from being linked to them. The priority was to set up a unit in which the nursing and clinical practices of terminal care could be established and then, through the Home Care and Teaching Services, be taken out to the local and wider communities. If the work at St Columba's was to be of any real and lasting value, every opportunity had to be provided for doctors, nurses and other health professionals from outwith the Hospice, in training, working in General Practice or hospitals to learn there. In this way hospice care could be taken into the home, general wards – wherever there was a need. Education had to be very high on the agenda. It was, "a sharing of a philosophy, almost a mission – affirming the importance of total care – but never to make them feel unable to do it themselves."

In the early days, courses and seminars were held in the children's classroom. The facilities were inadequate and make-shift, but it was important to get the teaching off the ground and to demonstrate that the professional staff at St Columba's wanted a partnership with their medical colleagues. Through it they could share their developing expertise. Many in the medical profession were sceptical of the idea of a Hospice and resented the implied criticism it represented. The doctors and nurses at the Hospice were entering a young discipline and there was a lot of work to be done. They had a broad strategy but what they had to go on initially was very little – their knowledge that dying patients and their relatives needed a better deal, an instinctive feeling of knowing that they could provide a service that would meet these needs and their experience of work in other hospices. Derek Doyle knew that he and his colleagues were embarking on important work that

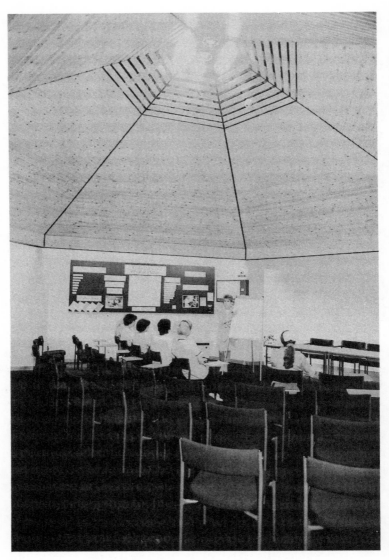

A teaching semmiar in the Birsay Hall.

would put them at the forefront of developing and refining pain and symptom control as well as providing a better way of caring. All this was yet to come and the term Palliative Care was hardly in use in 1977.

Most of the nursing staff who came to St Columba's in the early days came without any experience of hospice work. They had some experience of having nursed dying patients, although not necessarily good experience. Hospice staff received in-service training and courses were also developed over the years for nurses and doctors in practice elsewhere and for post-graduate and under-graduate students.

What young doctors hear when they visit St Columba's today is very different from the training and example given twenty years ago. Then, if there was nothing to be done for a patient, you walked on – not so much out of a lack of compassion, but because of helplessness in the face of death. Derek Doyle initiates young doctors in caring for terminally ill patients with a short, blunt introduction and throws them in at the deep end:

" 'I want to talk to you about God's greatest gifts'. That's when they shuffle uneasily because they all think I'm going to give them a spiritual lecture. Then I go on. 'The first is your bottom – learn to sit on it. The second one is ears – listen and, as you listen, the mouth remains shut. The eyes focus on patients' eyes and you will manage to sit still, listen, and keep the mouth shut. And for ten minutes show that person that they are the only person in the world that matters. I would say that the least important thing is to write out prescriptions, which you hold up so that you do not see the patient. You don't need to get near the patient!'. Having made these crude points, they've got it! Then I tell them to go and try it with a patient.

I take them to a patient and introduce them. 'Mrs X, this is so-and-so who's a medical student. Mrs X has very kindly agreed to tell you a story. OK, now shut up! You're not going to speak for ten minutes.' And they all come back and say, 'She was great fun, terribly interesting', and I have not asked them any chemistry or any drugs. They can all do that. They say, 'He's a fascinating man'. 'Yes – he's just like your Mum and Dad. That's someone else's mother or someone's father or someone else's girl-friend you were talking to. Now wasn't that easy?'"

It is all very different from the traditional induction of young doctors into medicine:

"You go to the first hall where there are forty bodies waiting to be dissected and woe betide you if you draw a breath or turn green! You're told that, 'It's just a body and as doctors you're going to see a lot of them.' In fact, you're desperately upset as you've never seen one before and it's ghastly. Compassion and sensitivity are programmed out of you in medical training. Many in Universities feel that you get the caring, nice, young students and they come out as know-all 'if only you were as clever as I am' types. What we are discovering is that, underneath it all, they are just as warm and caring and they are longing to have permission from the old men of Medicine to be themselves."

There is probably some good sense in teaching young men and women that, to be good doctors and good technicians, they must be emotionally detached; and there is probably good sense in the idea that, if they are emotionally uninvolved, then they are free to get on with the job. The idea of a surgeon shaking with distress as he contemplates making an incision would indeed drive patients away from the operating table. But in recent years there has been a feeling that things have gone too far, that the impersonal and detached attitude of many in the medical profession communicates a lack of caring and that the withholding of all emotion implies a lack of feeling. Caring that is given in this way devalues both the doctor and the patient. What young doctors can learn at the Hospice is that the ability to share in someone's grief does not necessarily overwhelm and incapacitate but gives enormous comfort; and that the sharing of human values gives strength, and courage, to both the patient and the doctor.

The word love is interchanged with compassion and used a lot in discussing caring. Love perhaps has a more personal ring to it but has become so devalued and sentimentalised in recent times that its use makes us uncomfortable. There is, in fact, nothing sentimental about love as it is shown and shared at the Hospice. Nor does it mean that all the staff get on with all the patients. When a patient is admitted to the Hospice there is no attempt to conceal anything, to hedge issues or deny what is happening, although it is usually the patient who knows the truth better than anyone. Facing this truth can be brutal. With the acknowledgement of it comes the responsibility to stay with the patient, to support him or her through the grief and anger at the loss of life. Love, in the real meaning of the word, is to do with this responsibility and honesty. This means a doctor or a nurse being able to say, "I find some of this awful. I've got to be honest and say I find some patients unpleasant and intolerable". It is easy to get confused about what compassion is. It took Derek Doyle a long time before he realised that it was all right to say that not all patients are pleasant and that it is safe to do that as long as it does not affect the patient – "You don't have to love everyone". It is easy to give to someone who is good, kind and caring. True compassion means giving, in spite of someone's shortcomings.

Derek Doyle makes much of truth and honesty, saying that doctors need to be honest about themselves – to admit their own shortcomings rather than pretending to have all the answers:

"We have to say, 'You are as vulnerable as anyone, but that is all right'. Being yourself means many things. It means for me to say to students, 'I don't know the answer. I understand your question but I don't know the answer to that. I'm not clever enough.' They all sit there and say. 'It's incredible he doesn't know.....!' We have to be honest in what we do."

In teaching, the Hospice doctors demonstrate these things informally, letting their students learn by seeing the

Men's TALKS

..., one of a group stood up at the end of a ... and thank ed them for what they had all learned:

... But, none of these things have been very important ... compared with wa ching you and Fred talking to patients. I've never ... what do e before. You got that chap in and, in a few minutes, there we tears of laughter running down his face. You two ... ... laughing too - it was like a 'Sundance act'. Then he was talking about dying and you were saying, 'hold on a minute, I'm not finished'. It was that sort of thing! And then we realised that in that time he had told us his life story, his fears about death, his broken marriages, about what he thinks about for the future. You told him about how you are going to help him. You told him at one point about how sad you were, you had a laugh, a few minutes later you had a tear in your eye."

All this is sometimes called "learning by osmosis". No, you cannot instil compassion. All Derek Doyle claims to do is "bring out" what is already there – which is educating in the real sense of the word. It is, in fact, simply teaching what is learned from listening to the dying:

"It is simple. There is love. Bring it out. You are saying to them, 'It is safe to be yourself. You've got a cool facade because you think you are distant from patients, but it is all right just to be yourself and you are not diminished by showing your humanity – you are bigger for it.'"

A 'SAFE' PLACE FOR PATIENTS

So what does all of this mean for the patients and their families? No-one can deny that there is a happy atmosphere in the Hospice. The staff are friendly, it is a place to sit and watch the world go by – what more could anyone want? It is so easy to be lulled into thinking that everything is wonderful and that death is somehow "good" here. Can death be "good"? The answer is that death comes in many different ways. No-one controls it and the reality is that there is pain and suffering, and it would be wrong to think that St Columba's is a place where people can have a "perfect" death. The idea appals those who work at the Hospice. It is sad but true that many people do believe that death can somehow be "sanitized". It is an attitude that offends many in the Hospice. Many do die peacefully. For others there is great struggle, despair and depression – but the purpose of Hospice care is not to deny anyone their anger and frustration. If anything, it is to allow patients and their relatives to experience, go through and express whatever their innermost feelings are – be it regret, despair or sheer rage. Some people go out kicking until the end – that is their right and no-one would try to take it away from them.

For this reason the Hospice has been described as "a safe place to suffer" and, whatever patients may be going through, the word they use most commonly to describe how they feel about the Hospice is "safe". What the Hospice offers most of all is a place where a person can die in their own way, whilst offering him or her as much relief and companionship as is possible.

The need to vent anger surfaces at times and a dying patient may need someone to shout at – how can a thirty-three year old not be angry? Hospice staff make it possible for that anger to come out because it needs to. Sometimes someone needs to say, "Why do you go on acting so calmly? Are you not furious inside?" Patients need to have the freedom to be themselves and the importance of hospice care is that it does everything it can to provide this freedom:

"We can make it possible for people to be as natural as possible in an unnatural environment. We make it freer for them by not imposing restrictions. You do not say, 'Don't say that in front of the doctor or use that language'. Being aware of patients' needs means that doctors and nurses react differently. Anger and frustration are accepted as such, rather than seen as inappropriate behaviour. "I went to see a patient and said, 'Hello' and was told, 'Go to Hell'. I asked the nurse what I had done wrong. She said, 'You could try asking him how he is'. I did and he replied that he was feeling awful and asked me if I wanted to know about that, and that is all it took!"

Studies of patients have shown that, while emotional torments are among the worst fears of the dying, physical pain and suffering and treatment are the most important. Patients worry that their pain and suffering will not be recognised. Derek Doyle says it is all too easy for a doctor to say to someone with chronic pain, "You look pretty well today". Patients worry too about inadequate pain control or wrong treatment. These worries are genuinely upsetting and evidence of the numbers of people who are on inadequate pain control show that such fears are not always groundless. Studies show that as many as thirty per cent of patients in general hospitals suffer poorly controlled pain. Getting pain and physical symptoms under control is the first priority when a patient is admitted. Physical and emotional worries are often bound up together. Patients may be anxious that nobody understands their fears or that their fears are not taken seriously, which is why listening and communicating are so important.

There is a fine line between meeting patients' needs and doing too much for them. Doing too much is the result of an over-caring and over-protective society and modern care systems can paralyse. "You care but you don't always have to be taking over. You have to let people experience things and live their lives – even the painful bits. One of the most difficult problems patients have to deal with is that of finding they are no longer needed. On the one hand, we want to care for them so that they have as good a time as they can in what's left to them. Here we have the families having to survive without them and, without admitting it, having to prepare for the time when they are not together any more. He's in here but she's got to get on running the household and the kids – life does go on without him. One bit of him is proud that she can do it and that she will somehow cope when he's not there. The other bit feels that 'she doesn't need me'. Ten o' clock at night is 'tear time' here. This is when he's likely to be saying 'She's just behaving so well but you'd think I was gone already'. Yet, what can she do? She can't come in here crying 'I can't cope'."

There is a lot of mention of courage on the part of the patients and families – but it is not the traditional sort of 'stiff upper lip' type of courage that is referred to. It is the courage of recognising the person behind the mask – the mask that so many of us wear in our attempt to hide our real selves from the world. People do it so effectively that many do not know their true selves until late in life. Often it is men that have most difficulty:

"It has struck me here that the big macho men who are really frightened and timid are so upset to discover this. They've never shown their real selves. We had a forty year old in, he had been a Commando – a paratrooper and he had killed. He said he had never thought about it. He had done thirty-nine jumps and said he had never been frightened of anything, but he was frightened now. He said he had never known fear until now. He analysed why. Up to this point in his life he could always deal with fear – 'You either put some more men in here or you fight over there or you machine-gun there. I was taught that if you know there's someone there and you can't see where – you fire. Here I know the enemy and I can't do anything and it's crowding in on me. To discover that I've been such a coward and that my wife is coping so well and running the whole show – making the decisions and everything is going smoothly – and I thought she was so fragile and needed protecting. I've just discovered that she knew I was a coward and she's been looking after me.' His wife was a little shy thing and she came in here, totally capable, and she would hold him in her arms soothing him and comforting him."

People gain all sorts of insights as death approaches and it can be very hard waking up to the life that might have been:

"People discover that they've got much more about them than they ever knew – the ones who say they did not know they had a skill or a gift and they could have used it".

These insights come too late and awareness of this kind

creates enormous regret of a wasted life. If they are able to pass on the importance of living life to the full to their children and others they leave behind, the lesson loses some of its sting.

Then there are those whose lives have simply been lacking in real happiness. "The saddest is the person who says at the end of their life, 'You know these last few weeks have been the happiest of my life'. To think they've got to sixty or seventy and the final happiness came at the end – what a waste of time." Patients come back from the brink of death and say everything has a new meaning. The ordinary things that are taken for granted or that go unnoticed become important again. They see how green the grass is, they smell the early morning dew and they hear children's laughter. They feel released from the constraints of being the person that they think the world wants them to be and are free simply to be themselves and free to enjoy life.

HOME FROM HOME

Jeanie Simpson, who took over after Dee Goldie as Nursing Director, has had a long involvement with the Hospice. She is a prize-winning general nurse, has an additional qualification in psychiatry and was further trained in management. Being attracted by the aims and ideals of the Hospice and interested in using her skills and qualifications in working with the terminally ill and the bereaved, she first applied for the post of Sister. Like her predecessors, whose portraits tell much about the women they were, she is a modern-style Matron to be found on the wards and at the bedside sharing in the care. She talks of the importance of the Hospice belonging to the patients:

"I think the patients that stand out – that you feel good about – are the ones that look on the Hospice as their home because they know they are not going anywhere from here – they are not able to go home for various reasons. Those patients I remember because they can make what is an

institution their home. My constant reminder is that this is the
patients' home – if they want to leave their magazines lying
about and their ashtrays full – fine! Patients in many ways are
encouraged to be themselves and not to be on their best
behaviour because they're in hospital. It's often said to them,
for example, if they don't like the lunch menu, then they can
ask for something different. We are very flexible and we try to
meet needs and that gives them a sense of security and
freedom. I think all these things help. If they had the choice,
home is where they'd be – not for all of them though. It isn't too
different from being at home here.

It is not just the environment that helps patients to be
themselves. It is the way in which the staff approach the
patients. It is a very caring place – you feel a great deal of love
directed to you as a patient. That allows you to relax and be at
home. There is a very natural gaiety. We do think it has a lot to
do with natural compassion that staff have – they're able to
spend time with patients – they're not rushing, or hassling.
Routines are very flexible."

Openness, honesty and freedom for the staff to express
their feelings all contribute to the atmosphere:

"We don't make it too difficult for the staff. It's a very
caring place – we don't go around with glum faces and it's not
forced. But there are times when morale is low in patients and
staff, because there's been a lot of deaths – that's unavoidable.
Patients are allowed to express that, staff are allowed to
express it. No one is hiding it. They talk about it. This makes
it different from a general hospital. No one moves from here
without patients knowing. If they've died, we say so. We had
a lady who died recently who looked on this place as her home.
I was quite involved with her – possibly more so than I
normally get the opportunity to be. I was the one who took her
to her home to get her things and she really felt this was her
home. She didn't have any close family. We were her family –
staff and other patients. She was the kind of lady who had
something for everyone. She was giving a lot to other patients

and staff without ever realising it. One morning I came in and she was unexpectedly unconscious. As soon as I walked in I knew something had happened because I felt everything was kind of flat. I went and saw her – she was dying. She died at lunch-time that day. Another patient whom she had become particularly friendly with was distraught by this. She could not bear the thought that she was going to lose her friend. We were able to sit down with her and to say that we were going to miss this lady too and that she had been very special to everyone".

ANGELS – BUT NOT SO DIFFERENT

The nurses who work at St Columba's are used to people saying, "Oh, I couldn't work there!" "Don't you find that very harrowing?" "How wonderful!" Given that all nurses have a particular quality which is a natural extension of the nurturing role, how special are the nurses?

"On the whole, the kind of staff drawn to this type of work, as well as being professionally qualified, are the kind of people who do not want to be cold, starched professional nurses – they want to be people and to share what patients are going through with them and help them as much as they can. I'm not saying they are more compassionate and caring than other nurses but they are more able to express it, and this environment allows and encourages them to – we'd be pretty horrified if it were not expressed."

To a large extent, there is a self-selection process that goes on although there have been mistakes in appointments. Anyone interested in saving souls is told there is no room for those who want to wade into what is considered a private area. There are also those who come thinking St Columba's will be a soft option because of the high staffing levels – the 'hand-on-the-fevered-brow' syndrome. Experience shows that these are the least able to cope with the emotional draining that goes with the job. The type of people who fit in well do not come complete with wings and halo. They have good qualifications, a normal home life which is their focus, but they also have an ability to "channel" the grief and distress of nursing the terminally ill:

"By the time they (patients) are in the Hospice, their life is a constant series of losses. Relatives are grieving too and you are at the end – part of it. The nurse who thinks that it will all be a very calm easy passage into the next life, while she sits and holds hands, is not the kind that can take on board all the emotions around her and channel them. These are the kinds of nurses and doctors we have – they can take all the distress and channel it. You do get someone who, by the nature of their personality, does not fit into the existing team. You get someone who, however hard they try, seems to rub people up the wrong way. If you make a wrong appointment in the nursing staff, it stands out within a month."

Clearly it is about a nurse being able to be involved, listen and cry with patients and relatives but without getting too involved in all the distress which is not always easy to do:

"You have angry patients or relatives, if they feel the diagnosis was missed initially. You have to be able to help patients channel usefully but without taking on all the emotion, the grief and the loss that is coming at you. Everyone has their own way of dealing with it. You can't take it all on board. You would be foolish to think you could. Very often it's a case of being there, listening, letting a patient shed it and not absorbing it. A certain amount of it will be absorbed because you can't listen to people in their sorrow and not feel any of it."

There are those that think that too much is made of the stress of working at the Hospice, particularly compared with a busy hospital where the difficulties for nurses working with the terminally ill are considerable. At the Hospice, the nurse-to-patient ratio, the pleasant surroundings and good working conditions make the job easier. They also create the right atmosphere for nurses to be able to support each other. In the early days it was thought that some means of dealing with the constant stress of working with terminally ill patients was needed and there were regular weekly meetings with a psychiatrist. It soon became apparent that the formality was inhibiting and, if a nurse or other member of staff had a problem, this was often the last place she would raise it. The system was abandoned and mutual support tends to be a spontaneous response that arises out of nurses being aware of each other's needs:

"Because of the nature of the people who come into this work, they care about people. They care about each other, which is one of the reasons why staff don't get into difficulties. They are supporting each other all of the time at different levels. People are available if trouble develops. The most difficult time for staff is if they are going through difficulties in their own life. Most of the time they can cope. Sometimes it all gets too much but I don't think we've had anyone depressed because of working here."

Because they care for each other, nurses have the same freedom to express what they might be feeling to one another, "You do get close to patients and when someone dies, you do feel that loss. You know if someone is having a bad time and you can just say, 'come on' and take them into the sluice room and just let them have a good cry and it's as simple as that."

THE HOSPICE IN THE HOME

While hospice philosophy is the same for the Home Care Team, the job of looking after patients at home is very different to looking after patients in the Hospice. To-day the Home Care Team are well-known in the city and highly regarded but getting the service off the ground was not without its problems. In the early days, there was suspicion and General Practitioners and Community Nurses were wary of the Home Care Service. There was concern that professionals might be at odds with one another over treatment. On the other hand many GPs, providing terminal care for patients at home, were interested in anything that would improve the quality of life for the patient and wanted to see what was on offer. They began by referring one or two patients to see how things would go. It was far from plain sailing – there was often antagonism and criticism at a time when the Hospice was new and not yet established in its own confidence. It took time to build trust and good working relationships. The ability to negotiate was, and remains, one of the key requirements of being a member of the Home Care Team. As well as relatives, General Practitioners and Community Nurses, there are also hospital teams all contributing to the on-going management of the patient's treatment.

The patients themselves retain far more autonomy as Home Care patients. They often make their own choice about whether to go along with a regime, whether to modify it or kick it altogether. Everything is geared differently to the Hospice environment – the professional is the guest in the patient's home, it takes time to build up trust and there may be considerable experimentation with treatment. Other professionals may suggest a different line from that of the Hospice. It all requires flexibility and co-operation. Meg McKenzie, Senior Home Care Sister since 1982, sees patience as all important to the professionals, even if they do believe they know what is best for the patient:

"We need to accept that the quality of life can be maintained while the regime and everything else is being experimented with.. There are other professionals who are loosely part of the team and we are all there to give the best possible service. Sometimes we have a bumpy journey watching a patient go through a process and knowing that process could be far more comfortable and far less painful if they would accept the routine. Often we are in a position where people are trying us out. In their own home they may be absolutely charming about going along with a routine but they think that the best way is to do without drugs. Or they say, 'I'll hold off until I really need these'. You say, 'Look we are anticipating pain so we keep on top of pain by continuing the regime'. It's endless explanation and negotiation. The contract is that you allow them to be individuals and you respect the choice they have made and you are simply there to be with them. There always has to be an opting out period for some people."

The aim of the Home Care Service has always been to facilitate people staying at home if this is what they want and what they and their families can handle. Material circumstances play only a very small part in this decision compared with whether patients see the home, the privacy of home and being with the people they love as important. With the help of the Community Nursing Service and the Marie Curie Sitter Service, it is possible to provide good support. If, on the other hand, there is an increasingly heavy burden, the Home Care Team may help the family to let go the responsibility and arrange for the patient to be admitted to the Hospice.

Whatever the differences for the staff looking after patients in the home, patients and families express the same sentiments as those in the Hospice – proving that it is not so much the place but the hospice care which is important:

"Relatives and patients find an inner strength as their confidence grows and they face a situation that they never in their lives dreamed they could tackle. Hospice care is about inviting individuals to be receptive and them growing in the reciprocity. It is a difficult thing to explain. It's clearly observable in some – tentative in others. As people let go the things that have been day-to-day worries, they gain more true freedom. It's knowing their own inner resources and taking responsibility for themselves. People at home are admirably able to take responsibility for themselves in ways that they never dreamed they could before. It's being in touch with the ground of their being. There is such a letting go of what they can no longer deal with themselves – they somehow grow as individuals. It's a beautiful process of someone becoming whole despite the fact that they are dying. It's the whole business of someone coming into being – because they have been hindered from the time they were born, by the so-called living that we do, until we come to this dying bit. It is a journey and people are invited to see that there are still tremendous possibilities, in the process we call the dying process, to actually live... and so frequently our society takes such a defeatist attitude to death."

VOLUNTEERS

As well as paid staff, there are all the volunteers who help to make the Hospice a "safe" place. Katharine Weir who organises a small army of four hundred or more points out that they are not "the blue rinse" brigade or what she calls the "hatted" volunteers from circles where it is considered socially acceptable to "do good". It irritates her that this myth is perpetuated. "Many of our volunteers are women who prefer not to work outside the home, many are on pensions. The majority are not grand at all. There are grey-haired ladies who get on and do a job quietly with no fuss". Volunteers come from all over Edinburgh and, while Katharine Weir is happy to have a volunteer from among the residents of Edinburgh's grand Georgian crescents, the majority come from the less grand parts of the city.

So how does a volunteer get drawn into the work? There is no one answer to that question but the underlying issues are summed up in one volunteer's story:

"I got involved because I heard that the Hospice were looking for people to raise money, so I joined a support group. There's always someone from Fife in the Hospice and that's where I come from. A general hospital isn't always the place to die. Most people want to be in homely surroundings. This place appealed to me because it was about families rather than individual patients. When I read about what the Hospice hoped to do, I wanted to get involved with a support group.

The more you know about this place the more you become involved. For five years I held jumble sales, coffee mornings, race evenings (when you ask your friends round to gamble on video'd horse-races), dinner dances, lunches for friends and stood inside ASDA with a tin. After that I felt that I had exploited my friends and run out of original ideas – it was time to go. Then I was asked if I would like to come and work at the Hospice so now I contribute in a different way.

When you're raising money you're removed from contact with the Hospice. Being here is different – it's a privilege to be allowed to work with the patients here. It's amazing how many retain their sense of humour. People are not really changed by what is happening to them. They are trying, under very difficult circumstances, to make the most of what's left. In a small way we can help them to be themselves. The Day Hospice patients can talk to us. We can listen. Sometimes they may speak to you in ways that they wouldn't speak to anyone else. You learn to touch people – hold their hands without embarrassment. It's comfortable. The more they talk to you, the more you can see them becoming comfortable with you – and you can see that patients give each other support. Many outsiders feel that people come here to die. In fact, people come here to live and make the most of what's left. You see people on a downward trend and then they find a reason for really living the last few days of their lives. We make a fuss of patients. We can make the difference between making it matter or it being terribly lonely and miserable.

There's a great deal of satisfaction, working here and you get a lot out of it. It's also a very humbling experience. I feel privileged but at the same time thankful that I am able to come. It's an area where I feel, in a small way, I have something to give. But I never feel blase about it – I take it seriously. I do feel the need when I have finished to go home and put it behind me. I come and I give what I can. The emotional involvement can be overwhelming and that's right! Unless you feel for the patients here, you have no right to be here. You can't be detached. It's partly to do with your age. You reach a point where people are your priorities not material things. I think I get a great deal out of being here – people talking to you about their lives helps you sort out your priorities. You see people change their attitudes about themselves. I remember one lady who came here very rejecting of herself because she was very disfigured. While she was here, with all the kindness, she began to feel special again and the change was wonderful. She was a lovely lady. I remember another man who told me that his wife woke him up every morning with a kiss saying 'I love you'. The awful thing was, all their married lives, they had been unable to say it. It was only at the end that they could. This sums it all up – a lot of people, especially in our culture, are so hesitant about expressing their real feelings ... just saying what they really feel."

Many people who come into contact with the Hospice through a death simply cannot resist the pull that it exerts and help in whatever way they can. When he first lost his wife, one man who is now a great supporter just wanted to put it all behind him:

"I remember when my wife died ... I was coming to and from the Hospice. Her condition gradually worsened and towards the end of the sixth week she lapsed into unconsciousness. I was here on the Wednesday. At five o'clock the next morning the telephone at my bedside rang and the night Sister asked me to come over. A tray with tea and toast was brought for me as I sat at Anne's bedside. When the end did come I was alone with Anne, as I had asked, but with all the help and support I needed within call. As I was coming away from the Hospice, the doctor said to me, 'You will come back and see us won't you?' I couldn't answer but I said to myself as I was driving home, 'I never want to see the Hospice again'. A few weeks later I was invited to attend a rededication service for the Hospice in a church in Edinburgh which was packed with hundreds of relatives, nurses and volunteers and I knew then that I would always go back."

CHRISTIAN IDEALS

Facing up to the reality of death does not mean there is no fear. Many people fear death and can be forgiven if they walk away from it. This is as true for the health professionals as the rest of us. It is beyond most individuals to make sense of it all. There are no easy answers to the age-old questions 'What's it all about?' 'Why are we here?' This is why the Christian ethic is important in the Hospice movement in general and is the corner-stone of St Columba's. Christianity has a view of life and death that gives meaning to both. Death is seen as part of life and the completion and fulfilment of it – each person's life being of value in its own right.

Yet while the Christian ethic was and remains the reason for providing the care in the first place, there are no conditions either on the staff or the patients to accept anything about religion or Christianity. Many staff do not have any fixed ideas or beliefs. They are simply caring people doing their best to do a good job. There has been a tendency to have active Christians in senior posts and at the beginning it was hoped that all the staff would have a Christian commitment. In practice this has been found to be too limiting. The Hospice is a professional unit and professional and clinical experience are important criteria in making appointments. The aim has been to get the balance right and great care has been taken to protect patients from people with too great a sense of vocation. The Hospice has attracted a fair share of religious zealots who came believing that they could save souls or convert from one religion to another. They very quickly discovered that the Hospice was not the place for them and they were asked to move on. This was more of a problem in the early days when rumours and misleading stories were rife – without ever having set foot in the place, many would have it that the

Hospice was some sort of holy place where nuns prayed over repenting patients.

Hospice staff have also been sensitive about protecting patients from those who see themselves as well-meaning but who want to use St Columba's and the patients for their own needs in other ways. Staff have learned to recognise people who are working out their own bereavements and their own losses. Now they have a policy of not taking on a volunteer within a year of bereavement. In their need to talk through their own problems, it would be all too easy for a volunteer to upset a patient. Derek Murray, who is now the full-time Chaplain, and the rest of the staff are realistic about what they can do and their limitations:

"We can only support patients and families. We're really not equipped as a counselling service for volunteers. We have had people who wanted to cling to us as their lifeline. At the beginning we wanted to be everything to everybody but we soon found out we just didn't have the time, the energy or the staff."

As for patients, it is irrelevant what faith they profess, to what denomination they belong or whether they claim to be agnostic or atheist. Not only is the Hospice lacking in any visible religious symbols, there is no proselytising or evangelising. The chapel is seen as important for those who want to make use of it for prayer or simply as a private place. Many patients do come to the Hospice wanting to make their peace with their God and do want spiritual support and guidance. They may want to talk over their fears and hopes with Derek Murray or the Anglican or Roman Catholic priest who assist him. Derek Murray is not easy to single out, since he does not parade his role with any obvious sign of a "man of the cloth" as he does his rounds to chat with the patients. As far as giving patients and relatives spiritual and practical support, he is down to earth about the role that he and his colleagues play. Like the medical and nursing care, support is based on the needs of patients and families. There is no attempt to intrude – he is simply there if they want anything from him. If a patient wants to enjoy the time that is left with a good book, a cigarette and the odd pint, believing that there is no hereafter, no one is going to disturb his right to these things:

"I catch people at the end of their lives, I catch them where they are. I don't know the whole history and it's not up to me to enquire unless they want to tell me."

He always introduces himself to patients and takes his cues from there. Those who do want to sort themselves out spiritually want to do it in their own quiet way and Derek Murray's approach is to use language familiar to them:

"A lot of people don't know the words to use. They fall back on the well-tried phrases of Granny's, or they go back to Sunday School days, or they simply squeeze my hand – a lot goes on without it being put into words. That's why we have a communion service. I don't think people are here to hear sermons."

The lack of a sermon at these services highlights the fact that the ministry here is not about preaching to people. The emphasis is always on what is important to the patient or relative:

"A lot of folk can't really say, 'I want to believe as a Christian', or 'I want to put my trust in Christ.' But they can say, 'I can take a piece of bread and I can take a sip of wine and I know what that means.' Or we can say the Lord's Prayer together and they can do that – we do get people who haven't ever done that before. We had an old man in the Day Hospice who always came to prayers and then came to communion and at the end he was in tears – he had never had communion before. He had never had the opportunity to join a church."

Those who are church members are looked after by their own minister or priest. The patients who look to Derek Murray for help are those who have not been to church in a long time, but who know they need someone to bury them. They may have drifted away from their church or never been invited to join a church when they moved house. About half of the patients have some kind of church connection although they are not necessarily church-goers. Many say they have "no religion" meaning that they have not been to church for a long time. While quite a number describe themselves as agnostics, only a few claim to be atheists. Edinburgh is a multi-racial community and there are no bars to people of different ethnic origins or religious backgrounds making use of the Hospice services. There have been Jewish, Muslim, Sikh and Buddhist patients there.

The lack of religious symbolism and the acceptance of patients of all faiths and beliefs is part and parcel of the philosophy that puts patients and their needs first. Derek Murray sees it also as a particularly Scottish trait:

"It's mainly in the English Hospices that they go in for religious symbolism and prayers on the wards. It's a more public religion and some English trained staff resented the lack of it here. There's a kind of Scottish reticence that says you do your religion at home and in church, but you must never force it on everyone. So we never got very far with ward prayers. We wouldn't want prayers over the loudspeakers with patients having to dive under the blankets to escape them. There are Hospices where religion is very 'up-front' and, although we have the chapel here, we have always felt that we shouldn't push it at people."

Many of the conventions that people have happily flouted in their youth sometimes become important at the end of life. People may have regrets that they were never baptised or, if they have lived with someone, that they never married. People can and do set these things right. One patient wanted to make "an honest woman" of his "bidie-in" of many years standing. Derek Murray is at pains to point out that the couple were perfectly happy and there was no pressure from him or anyone else. Another patient wanted to see her son married before she died. She had her wish and her son's wedding was held in the Hospice itself with his own teenage children present. She died the following week, content to have been at this important event in her son's life.

PATIENTS

Patients, many of whom come and go for some time, will tell you that they enjoy the company in the Day Hospice. They meet new people, make friends and enjoy the social activities and outings. They will tell you, as Derek Doyle says, that they "feel safe" or that they are happy and content. Or they may talk about the way their lives have changed as a result of serious illness. While it is the illness itself that leads to people reassessing themselves and their lives, it is often contact with other patients in a similar situation and understanding staff who help with this process. Jim, who worked for a brewery before he was diagnosed as having cancer at the age of forty-seven, felt that the Hospice had a considerable impact on his life:

"St Columba's got me going again. I thought of it as people dying. I thought I'd give it a try. It was well known for cancer. I thought I wouldn't have to come back if I didn't like it, but I don't know what I'd do without it now. I'd have long, lonely days, with no-one to talk to. I feel much better getting out and meeting people. Having people to talk to – that's important and I have friends here. It's made a big difference to me. My nerves were bad. Now I feel more relaxed. You realise you are not the only one. A lot of people are worse off than you. The company is good. I've learned to make things and paint. I'm learning things I've never done before. I never had time for hobbies and making things. I used to have a good social life. I was never in the house. I was out at the pub or bowling. Here I've made friends with patients, helpers and staff. They are all very nice. It is surprising how many good people there are. I look forward to coming here. My illness changed my whole life – no bowling, no work. I've always worked. Being here, I'm more content than I would be. I'm more understanding of people. I make allowances for people and accept them as they are – that's a big change in me. I wasn't very tolerant! You can talk about problems here.

My mates have a different attitude to St Columba's now. They see what it is really like here and now they know what they are giving for. Since I've been here they've organised a raffle. I don't get down or depressed, or if I do it's never a deep depression. I get depressed if I'm on my own too much."

Jim described how being with other people had changed not only his attitudes and expectations about life and death, but those of his friends as well:

"People were embarrassed at first when they heard I had cancer. They didn't know what to say. They treated me as special at first. Some of my mates wouldn't come and see me. They thought I would just be lying in bed. Now they've got used to me and they treat me normally. I think my mates were expecting me to go soon. They've changed their attitude and say things like, 'You're looking well'. I'm not frightened of dying. I'm realistic. We all know we are going to die but we don't know when. I might not die of cancer. I could die of a heart attack or be killed in a car accident – that could happen to anyone. It puts things into perspective when you think like this.

Your attitude is important and that comes from what you know about other people. I would have said that people with cancer expect to go quick. I had a cousin who had a lump. She knew she had it but wouldn't go to the doctor because she was feared to. She died soon after being told she had cancer. But I've met people in here who've been coming for a long time. Andrew's been coming here for over a year. It changes your attitude."

Patients who come into the Hospice are from all walks of life but there is nothing to suggest that the differences between people create barriers. People are accepted for who they are and the kindnesses they do:

"There's a mixed bunch of people here. At first you might

think some of the helpers are a bit.... you know, maybe a bit better than ordinary folk. I maybe thought that at first but then I didnae believe somebody would come and pick me up and do that for me. But there's no, 'they're one class and I'm another'. I come from Leith and we're maybe a bit coarser talking but not rough. You're not made to feel different. It is amazing how many good people there are here."

As Derek Murray says, many of the people who come to the Hospice describe themselves as, "not very religious", or they say they are a Christian but not a church-goer. Having a terminal illness does not necessarily change these views and, while the chapel is an important reminder of Christian values, what really matters to many patients is the practical expression of them:

"I come to the services here but I'm not really a church-goer and I don't get a lot out of it. The chapel isn't that important to me and it wouldn't matter if it wasn't here. It's the people that matter. Everybody is so good to you. They don't ram religion down your throat – you don't have to have anything to do with it. You are free to take or leave it. I see a lot of the minister. He's very chatty but he doesn't talk about religion all the time."

For others the chapel is a haven to escape to and where batteries can be recharged:

"The chapel is so peaceful. I let my mind float. I don't think about anything, I just let it all go. It's all part and parcel of this peaceful existence. In hospitals they don't seem to realise that you need that as well. Being in bed and fed pills is what they think you want. They do not realise that you need a bit of human kindness, your hand held and somewhere nice and quiet to go. Here they realise it is very important and you can draw an inner strength from it – use your own resources. A hospital doesn't encourage you to do that at all. With cancer it is very important to draw on your inner resources and they encourage you to do that here, everywhere you go. Doctors here don't talk about fostering inner resources but it is recognised. I think that's why there are all these quiet places. Inner resources have played a big role in my being able to cope. I feel strong and more determined. There is no reason why I can't stay alive for another three or four years. They don't put time limits on you here – you've got five years, three months. Where are you supposed to get confidence and comfort from that? Here they say you can live as long as you want. You can go up to the chapel – take rest up at the chapel. There is a minister who walks about and will sit down and talk to you – not as a priest or chaplain but as a man. They seem to know instinctively the right sort of thing to say. Rather than the negative approach, 'Are you feeling better?' they say, 'I can see you look better today, you must be better'. You need a lift when you are feeling down."

Much is made of the way in which patients benefit from the lack of tight routines compared to hospitals. This same patient, a woman in her early forties, described how the way she was treated at St Columba's allayed her fear of pain and discomfort:

"Hospital-wise it is quite different from anything I've been in before. They have a completely different way here. Their idea is pain is not something you have to bear, you can control it and quickly. The staff here are capable of giving pain control immediately. They don't have staff on the floor who have to go and get permission from somebody else. You're not waiting around for hours and hours as you do in hospital. I've waited maybe two hours for an injection. They really have quite a different attitude. Anything I've had that I don't think is working, they don't insist on giving it to you. Hospitals decide you are going to have it even if it makes you sick. I think it's a pity that you have to be treated like that when there are places like this where you can be treated with dignity. Your feelings are considered all of the time – first and never second. This surprised me.

It was my own doctor who suggested that I needed a rest and St Columba's would be the best place – a Hospice that

understood all the ins and outs of it and all the drugs, good,
bad, new, old, in use – all the methods in use. I came in for four
pints of blood. They were very good about it. They said there
were platelets in my blood but I didn't understand what that
meant. Did it mean that I couldn't have a blood transfusion, or
what? Off they went and got a doctor and he explained
everything clearly. They don't have time to explain in hospital
or they just aren't in the habit of explaining. I am terrified of
needles in my arm. It's silly, just a thing, I just don't like the
look of blood. They didn't say, 'Oh, for goodness sake, you're
an adult, behave yourself'. They went away and got a bag to
cover the blood bag so I couldn't see it and bandaged up the
needles. They made everything so easy – they never made me
feel I had made a fuss about nothing. All they were concerned
about was that I had a problem about what they were doing.
It had to be done so what was the easiest way of doing it? It took
fear away. They gave me a cup of tea and held my hand. They
said my GP will be written to and be given all the information
on what is happening here.

It builds your confidence in as much as you're left a lot in
control. You have the ability to say, 'No, I don't want that', to
any treatment. They never give orders. They make
suggestions. I'm comparing it with a blood transfusion in
hospital at Christmas. I went in with a temperature. The doctor
was young and flustered. I was hysterical as he couldn't get the
needle into my arm. The sister in charge said, 'Go away, I'll do
it'. It doesn't give you a lot of confidence and I could see this
bag of blood. I had told them it made me feel physically sick
but they didn't do anything about it. Here I had a toilet I could
get back and forward to. There I was given a commode by my
bed. Then the sister came on duty and said that was not where
commodes belong and would they all please be put back. That
frightened me – that something would happen that I couldn't
control. Not only did I have this bag of blood and a needle in
my arm that I could see, I had no way of getting to the toilet
other than calling a nurse and waiting until she came. I had to

be taken to the toilet. They made no provision for the fact that I might not make it, no covering on me, no towel or commode. I found it humiliating and thoughtless. In hospitals they all have to get permission. It is difficult not to be critical of hospitals. I know they are doing their best and they do try. A lot of the time they seem rushed off their feet – they are so busy that they haven't time to give you all the attention that you get here. They seem under-staffed but for someone like me, who's got cancer, there's a world of difference – but it's the system that's at fault, not the people. You go for an appointment at Out-Patient's, it says eleven o'clock but that means nothing. Whereas when the doctor here says two o'clock, he'll arrive promptly. It makes a big difference – your life is your life. Clinic places are quite depressing.

Little things are so important. I'm a vegetarian and they always have tons of vegetarian food here and that makes a big difference – that they bother to give you food that you like. And it's lovely when a pretty wee nurse pops in and chats for five minutes – has the time to spare – just general chit-chat. They all want you to live. You can feel it – and they want you to go home and come back again. That is the difference between hospice and hospital. They have a very positive attitude, quite different to just being fed with drugs to keep you pain-free until you die.

They tell you to let them know straight away when you want anything. Last night I had been crying – I had a pain and the doctor came and said, 'How long have you been crying?' 'Not long', I said. 'They had started drug rounds and I didn't want to interrupt'. He said that was all very well but the whole point of this place is treatment is immediate. They tell us that when we come in – ring the bell and tell them what you want.

I think cancer has to be approached in a slightly different manner – anything that goes into remission – MS, any of these diseases – should be approached in the manner they approach it here. I've been to the Bristol Cancer Clinic and been treated by a Homoeopathic doctor and they've all made this clear.

The doctors here aren't negative about it, but the doctors in the hospital didn't agree with it at all – they laughed at it. My own doctor encouraged it. The specialist who gave me three months to live came around when I was in getting my first transfusion and said, 'Well gentlemen, this just goes to prove one should never be dogmatic. You should always look at the patient's and person's will to live first'. It is difficult to change attitudes of people like this but here I don't have to fight them. You could say, 'There is no reason why I have to die of this disease tomorrow – I could do x amount of things to help myself.' We all know we have got cancer and we know we are going to die, but here we can die in our own time, in our own way."

In the end people do die in their own way and, as is so often said, they all find the courage – as if all the 'letting go' that is talked about in the weeks before frees them. Many do it in their own good time – delaying, putting off the time, waiting for the right time or to see something completed. There are stories like the one about Archie. He was a man in his late fifties who had carcinoma of the face and was less than a pretty sight. But his cheerful disposition made him popular with everyone and, being a keen bowler, he managed several nights out with the boys even though he was on high doses of morphine. During his time at the Hospice he made raffia stools in the Day Hospice to raise funds. The orders kept coming and Archie simply refused to die until he had completed them. Eventually the order-book was clear and Archie died easily and peacefully. Bill is remembered because of the effort he put into staying alive until he had seen his only daughter once more before he died. Towards the end, with very little time left, it looked as though this was not to be. Knowing what it meant to both of them and desperately trying to get through to the old man, who was slightly deaf, all Derek Doyle could do was to shout into his ear "You can't go yet". It worked. Bill did hang on and he did see his daughter.

Death can be a relief and a release for both patient and

relatives and, though there is great sadness, there is often consolation. For relatives and staff, consolation may be difficult to find when the death is that of a young person or a young mother or father. There are times when the grief is beyond comprehension and faith is stretched to its limits and there is little or no comfort. Doctors and nurses will tell you that it is the courage of patients that keeps them going, as one of the volunteer Hospice doctors described:

"I remember a young mother here with young children and she sat there with her eighteen-month old on her knee and looked at the child and said, 'You are too young for your mother to die, aren't you?' It was unutterable grief. You wonder how people cope with unutterable grief .... but they do."

"Courage" is one of the most frequently used words when doctors, chaplains and nurses speak of patients at the very end of life. It is almost as if people are given courage. It comes to everyone in the end. Even those who think "I'll never be like that" are proven wrong. There are the frail old ladies, perhaps long since widowed or never married, who throughout their lives have been very undemanding and get on with dying in much the same way – still giving with a smile, a gentle word. Then there are the younger patients, with ambitions and dreams that will never be fulfilled, needing courage to do what they can in the time left:

"Yes, there are times when the fear of death recedes and people are freed up to do things. I remember one patient – a woman with two young daughters of twelve and fourteen. She took a dip and realised that she hadn't long. Her daughters came in to visit and she took them aside and went through all the things they needed to know to cope with life – emotions, how to cope with boyfriends. She showed enormous courage but she wanted to complete the job. When death comes it can often be a kind of gentle death."

Those who work with the terminally ill say that the dying give so much to them – that it is about human relationships and sharing and that, so often, it is the dying who comfort the living:

"It sometimes means standing at the bedside and crying, like last night I went to the bedside of a lady and told the staff I knew her well, I would comfort her. I went into the room and within three minutes I was holding her and there were tears running down my face. I suddenly realised she wasn't crying, she was comforting me. She said afterwards, 'Isn't it wonderful to have people who care?'.".

The doctors, chaplains and the nurses will tell you that people are rarely frightened of death nor are they frightened of being damned for what they did in this life. They may be afraid of the letting go of life. How can people in the Hospice help at times like this? How does a nurse sit with a dying patient? Why is she not paralysed by her own fear? There are no lessons in what to say. Joan Cooper feels that many of the nurses and the doctors at the Hospice are comfortable with the work and are able to do it with a sense of ease as well as involvement because they have faced up to their own mortality. She says sitting with and talking with dying patients is a matter of trusting your instincts and that, "God puts the right words into your mouth". If a patient is well cared for and looked after properly, death is not terrifying but a natural process of living. More important than anything is simply communicating – both listening and talking with a dying patient:

"If you can talk with the patient, not at them, the words do come to you. You mustn't evade the issue. We think it's a terrible thing to die, when we all know we can't go on living forever – and who wants to? But there are words of comfort that you can offer. You can simply say, 'think of all the people who have taken that step before you', and I think that gives people the courage they need."

THE HOSPICE EXPERIENCE

THE VISITOR

There are many people who, never having visited, think of St Columba's as some sort of religious institution or holy place. They expect a quiet cloistered atmosphere, nurses moving silently from bed to bed speaking in hushed tones and an air of despair and gloom. In fact, nothing could be further from the everyday life of the Hospice.

A visitor at the Hospice finds himself in lovely grounds with the elegant facade of Challenger Lodge situated between the two major developments of the nursing wing to the left and the teaching wing to the right. Originally known as Wardie Lodge, the house was built by Playfair in 1825 and was the home of the Misses Hope who were keen horticulturalists. They laid out the garden at the front of the house with rare shrubs and trees. The ground at the back falls away steeply down to the shore and several of the rooms have wonderful views overlooking the sea. In 1889 it was bought and renamed Challenger Lodge by Sir John Murray. Sir John was a naturalist and scientist who was a member of a four year round-the-world expedition to explore the Atlantic, Pacific and Indian Oceans. HMS Challenger was the three masted wooden sailing ship, with an auxiliary steam engine, in which he had made the voyage. In 1929 the house became a children's home opened by the Edinburgh Cripple and Invalid Aid Society. Over the years it was a convalescent home for children recovering from polio or infantile paralysis as it was known then. When it was purchased by the Hospice, Challenger Lodge was still a home for children in need of care.

In the sixties it was also the home for "Greyfriar's Bobby", the much loved character from the film of the same name, who was presented to the children of Challenger Lodge by the film company.

Entering by the house itself, the visitor arrives in the elegant reception hall. Hospuss, the Hospice cat, sleeps contentedly in the sun that streams through the cupola. Immediately facing is the chapel. On a warm summer's day the room is cool and fresh. Through the windows there are views of flotillas of small yachts, braced against the winds and tides of the Firth of Forth. The atmosphere is peaceful and relaxed and not tense or sombre or heavy.

Down the corridor, which joins Challenger Lodge to the nursing wing, is the Day Hospice. A group of patients is enjoying being entertained by a professional singer – singing along to some of the old favourites. Further on, in the hairdresser's room, an elderly lady is having a shampoo and set, insisting that the style is not too "bouffant" and as she wants it for when her visitors arrive.

In the nursing wing are four main rooms which each take a number of patients although there are also some single rooms. There is a bustle of activity and good natured chit-chat between patients and staff. The rooms are light and airy and fresh flowers, donated or bought from the flower fund, add colour and life to every corner. At the side of the beds are more flowers and a welcoming card with the patient's name. There is no rigid routine with scheduled doctors' rounds. Doctors come and go throughout the day. While it may not be a five star hotel (some patients will tell you otherwise) lunch is what the patient wants and can eat. Today there is poached salmon followed by ice-cream but, if that's unpalatable, the cooks do their best to accommodate different tastes.

The ward opens onto the verandah, where groups of patients and visitors are deep in conversation and children play. Over in the corner, a pretty white-haired lady is relaxing in one of the comfortable armchairs. A nurse tucks a rug over her as she settles down to read cards from family and friends. The chaplain stops to chat to an elderly gentleman. The chances are that he is not a church-goer but he enjoys the company and exchanging jokes. By the window a couple sit holding hands, like two young people very much in love for the first time. The moment holds both enormous happiness and great sadness and you are reminded that the only thing that is in short supply here is time.

An elderly lady of ninety-two is helped into a chair. Her body is thin and frail and wasted, but her face is full of life. A doctor arrives. He beams at her and says, "Hello", kneels down and leans on the armchair and takes her hand. Perhaps he is going to pray with her, but the laughter is not quite appropriate. Then you realise that she has poor vision and the perfectly natural gesture of kneeling, which is neither contrived nor patronising, is simply to make conversation between them easier. She boasts to the doctor that she managed to walk that morning and he surprises her by saying, "I know, I saw you". They both laugh – both amused that she still has some 'get-up-and-go' and both pleased to be sharing the thought.

The flower ladies go about their business without intruding on the groups of visitors around the beds. Displays are carefully re-arranged and sprayed with water. Today there is a shortage of flowers. As she does her best for the men's ward with the leftovers, one of the ladies mutters, "I wish people would realise men like flowers too!". You note how right she is and that many people forget this or play safe with a box of chocolates for fear of offending. Two small children ask for a vase for the flowers they have brought for their Granny. It is February and there are splashes of bright yellow everywhere, reminding you that winter is almost over and spring is not far away. The daffodils and the small children lift your spirits and you realise that hope springs eternal in the human breast for good reasons – there are beginnings as well as endings and life goes on.

'ANGELS IN DISGUISE'

For the most part the flowers, tea and poached salmon are indeed luxuries to be enjoyed and there is no reason why it should be otherwise. But these things are 'the icing on the cake'. Patients come here to have pain and symptoms controlled. Many are admitted at the end of a long period of illness and struggle that may have involved them in distressing treatment. They are often very weak, low in spirits and in considerable pain. The priority for the doctors is to get the pain under control. There is no pretence that cure is an option and emphasis is on care. The Hospice does not claim to work miracles and it can take a little time and patience before a patient is comfortable. Patients' symptoms are often exaggerated because of anxiety. Loneliness and isolation can make pain far worse. So too can the fear of pain. These patients can be nursed back to a better state of health and, with physiotherapy, helped to walk after being bedridden for some time.

At any one time there are as many as thirty patients. Doctors and nurses very quickly get to know them. Everyone is given the same care and consideration. They are treated as individuals and as people with families and never as cases. Nurses come on duty at three different times in the day and each shift begins with a detailed briefing on every patient by the Sister in charge. The briefing covers not only what drug treatment the patient is on and what other treatment may be required but also whether he or she is in good spirits. "Mrs Brown, Ca cervix, had a good night. She slept well after being given night sedation and woke hungry – she ate breakfast and says she would like to sit on the verandah this morning." "Mrs Jones, Ca lung, slept fitfully, was given a change of position at 4 am, but is quite poorly this morning. Her colour is not good and she has bad pressure sores. She will need bowel treatment this morning." A note is also made of anything that happened that may have lifted spirits. "Mrs Brown spent the day with her daughter. She came back very tired but had a wonderful time." Sister mentions a patient's wife and how she is coping and that the nurses should keep an eye on her, "Mrs Jenkins has slept

Dr Alison Gordon with a patient, 1986.

The domestic staff coming off duty.

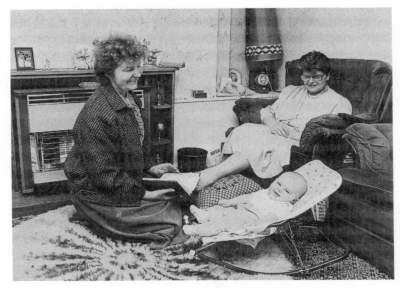

Sister Meg McKenzie with patient in her home.

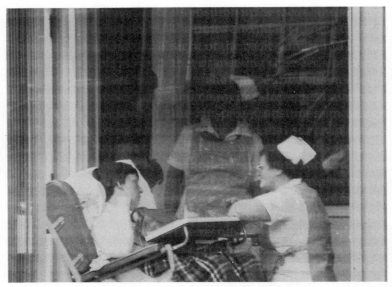

Nurses with a patient on the verandah.

in an armchair in the ward for the past three nights and she's exhausted". The acceptance of death and the readiness for it as the quality of life deteriorates is also reflected in the Sister's comments and observations, "Mrs McDonald is just very weary and feels it's all taking a long time. She needed someone to sit with her last night and she's still sleeping".

The ward round begins after the briefing. Bed baths, commodes, bowel treatments and mouth cleaning may sound very down-to-earth, but this is what caring is about. If a patient is in pain or discomfort from being constipated, then treatment to relieve this is often more important than anything else.

The nurses work in teams. There is a lot of chatter among nurses and patients. Beds are made and patients lifted into comfortable positions. Lifting, a great part of the nurses' work, has become an art. "Can you do an Australian?", asks one young nurse of an inexperienced auxiliary who looks blankly at her and wonders if it's something to do with turning upside down. Planting one foot on the floor and a knee on the bed she proceeds to demonstrate. She lowers her back (the most vulnerable part of a nurse's anatomy) and weaves her arms round the patient, whilst somehow managing to support her with her shoulder. Together the two of them gently 'shunt' the patient up the bed to a more comfortable position. He heaves a sigh of relief and settles himself.

A cleaning lady, who has quietly given long years of service to the Hospice, is busily vacuuming every nook and cranny with the air of someone who knows her job is ordinary but no less important for that. She stops to admire the photograph of grandchildren by a patient's bed and they proudly exchange stories of their families. Mollie was a clippie on the buses for twenty years. She was up at 4am every day. Both women have worked hard for their children. They wanted them to get on in life, have some of the things they did not and, in turn, the children, have not let them down. Standing on tiptoes, the cleaning lady dusts parts that others would not bother to reach and gets on with the job like a good old fashioned house-wife who knows instinctively that "cleanliness is next to Godliness".

Behind a curtain, the noisy clatter of a bedpan signals some sort of disaster. A commode has fallen apart and some of the patients proceed to do likewise – with laughter. The rear end of a nurse appears from beneath the curtain as she mops up the spilled contents. There is more laughter and rude (but complimentary) comments about her anatomy from the patients in the opposite beds. It all goes to show that nothing (and perhaps men's sense of humour in particular) changes that much. People can still see the funny side of life and all the gaiety that is spoken about is normal everyday banter.

The gentleman in Room Three needs help with getting off the commode. He is tired and weary and the effort of moving him back into bed drains his strength further. While he rests back to recover, he groans quietly at his own helplessness and dependence. One of the nurses strokes his head gently, takes his hand in hers and holds it for a moment or two. He is a grown man but both know that he is hurting for many reasons and the touch gives something that drugs and medicines cannot.

In the bed at the end of Room One, a patient lies sleeping. A nurse gently tries to wake her and explains that she is going to roll her over and spray her bottom. Her pressure or bed sores are raw and painful. The patient is too ill and weak to move herself and keeping her comfortable means that her position has to be changed regularly. Sheepskins and special mattresses help but bed-sores are a constant problem for the bed-bound.

A Sister goes through to the little private room to sit and talk with a patient's wife. She is worried about the children and how she will cope without her husband but cannot talk to him about her worries. At this point they both have different needs – he is coming to terms with not seeing his children grow up and she is anxious about how she will manage on her own. As long as they both need comforting, they cannot reassure each other and it falls to the nurses, doctors and chaplain to help them to the point of acceptance. When he can see that having loved his children means that he is with them forever, and when she realises that she has the strength to carry on without him, they will be able to be close.

A middle-aged lady who has come to see her old friend, May, wishes that she had not. She is shocked to see how thin and gaunt May is and says that she would prefer to remember her as she used to be. The young nurse, wise beyond her years, tells her how pleased May was to see her, that it brightened up her day and that these memories will fade and she will remember the good things as well as these sad times.

At 9 pm the night nurses take over for a ten hour shift. By midnight most patients are settled and asleep. Patients' wives and husbands are to be found camping on armchairs next to beds undisturbed by the hum of the Mediscus bed. The Mediscus bed is a wonderful invention that looks like lots of miniature inflatable mattresses side by side. Sleeping on it is like floating on air and gives relief from pressure sores. Despite the constant drone, the patient is fast asleep and you hope that in her dreams she is drifting in some tropical lagoon.

An elderly gentleman is anxious and a nurse goes to sit with him. Two hours later she is still there and one of her colleagues goes to take her place at the bedside. At 5am in the morning the comforting smell of tea and toast wafts up the corridor and it's time for a break.

Two of the nurses who have been at the Hospice from the beginning reminisce about the early days. Among the things they miss most of all is the family atmosphere – the way things used to be when the Hospice was smaller. They worry about all the teaching and whether it takes away from the patients in some way; they are not sure about the nurses who come from general hospitals bringing starched efficiency and who are not, as they see it, too tuned in to what the Hospice is about. It is another reminder that nothing stays the same and 'letting go' is a part of everyday life that we all find hard, simply because we do not have much faith in the future being better. The importance of teaching and making Hospice care available in other units is discussed. Five o'clock in the morning is not the time for complex arguments and the matter seems very simple. It is hard to see how the teaching could be more important than patients – without the care in the Hospice there would be nothing to teach. As for the new young nurses, they are bright, professional and caring and they want to be at the bedside giving the care – which is what nursing is all about.

At 6.45 in the morning one of the patients dies. Her two daughters have been with her throughout the night. She has been here for ten days. For the first few days she was quiet and subdued, but her frustration erupted into a storm of anger and protest three days ago. She swore loudly at the nurses, demanded a telephone, demanded a bath and stood her ground with all the defiance she could muster. The four letter words jarred in the quiet room but something said, "Let her shout and rant and rave. Let her vent her anger, let her scream at her God if that is what she wants to do". With the anger and passion spent, she sat on the bed where a nurse held her in her arms. She confessed to the nurse that she knew, "Something was happening and she was fighting it too much". Tired and exhausted from the outburst, she slept with the nurse by her side for the rest of the morning. The day before she died she was peaceful and calm. Her daughters stayed with her throughout the day and the night. With death came the release from suffering.

The family stay for a while. Then she is taken through to the room where the nurses carry out the last offices of laying out. Nothing changes here. Speaking to the patient in the same way the nurses gently wash the worn body. "I'm just going to give your face a wash, Mary, and I'll be very gentle." "A nice clean nightie – this is a pretty pink." With the same care, yet knowing she is beyond pain, they change the clothes and the bed linen and finally let her be. There is no more distress, no despair and nothing to fear – only a sense of a life completed.

When all the last details have been attended to, Mary is taken into the sanctuary and placed in the bed there. One of the nurses puts flowers on the pillow. The pale oak cross hanging on the wall is a simple reminder of the source of all life and love; and the early morning sunshine, streaming through the stained-glass window, seems to lighten the weight of the all-night vigil for both Mary and the nurses who shared it with her and her family. When the daughters return she looks peaceful. She will stay in the care of the Hospice right until the end, when a nurse hands her body over to a funeral director; and she will be treated with the same love, respect and dignity that has been given to her in her last week of life.

Between them, the daughters have nursed their mother over a long period of time. Managing households, jobs and children of their own, they have gone backwards and forwards to cook, clean and take care of her. The difficult bit for both of them was being unable to do it right to the end. Why are people so hard on themselves? She knew what good daughters she had and that, when the time came, St Columba's was the right place. There were nurses to move her, medicines when she needed them and ample supplies of fresh sheets if, as often happens, she lost control of bodily functions. She could accept this care knowing that it freed her just to be with her daughters. Now there is simply a great void where, until a few hours ago, their mother was. But it is clear to see that there is a close bond between the two women and they will be a strong support for each other through the funeral and in the months to come.

An auxiliary nurse who is new to the Hospice looks close to tears. Another nurse puts her arm around her shoulder and steers her aside where she cries realising that she feels the loss too. No matter that it happens often, when someone dies everyone feels a sense of loss and everyone is touched. The strong support those who are feeling the strain today so that they will be the strong ones tomorrow. No-one is a constant "tower of strength" because caring is a tiring business and everyone has days when they are exhausted.

Despite all the talk of the Christian faith, the religious symbols, that many expect, are no-where in evidence. What is important is the caring – whatever the faith of the person giving or receiving it – and it is to be seen and heard and experienced by all. It is in the thought and attention that have gone into creating the right environment, the time freely given by the tea and flower ladies, the shared jokes, the gentle shifting of a patient to a more comfortable position. There are a thousand small ways in which care is shown by everyone on the ward.

While there is much activity and bustle, this is not the place for briskness. Briskness smacks of "we'll have you up and about in no time". That is the way of hospitals – not because the staff are uncaring but because their job is to move people on, get them well, and back into the mainstream of life. Briskness is about hurrying on to the next thing to be done. It is about the way so many of us live our everyday lives. We hurry to finish this so we can get on with that, often forgetting to stop and enjoy the moment – the present – where life is. Walking into the Hospice gives a sense of peace and calm. Here the imminence of death seems to give meaning to life.

There is also this strong sense of community in the Hospice and a sense that everyone is sharing in what goes on – patients, staff and families. There is little standing on ceremony and no-one is aloof or puts on airs-and-graces. There is an acceptance of death from those who are doing the caring and those who are being cared for. It is not only the patients who are facing up to the difficult questions about death that most of us brush aside. This is perhaps why those doing the caring do not see themselves as separate from the terminally ill. They see themselves simply at a different stage of life. The recognition of death creates the environment that seems to free people to live lives that are more in tune with their own needs and the needs of others. What matters most here is the present. The past is all memories and the future is unknown. This is true for everyone at the Hospice – not just the patients. Because there is no urgency and no hurrying, only the need to deal with the everyday things of life, you see and hear gestures of caring and affection that have the enduring quality of love.

LIVING IN THE REAL WORLD

THE BUSINESS OF RUNNING THE HOSPICE

Within Challenger Lodge is a warren of small rooms where administrative staff deal with the day-to-day running of the Hospice – from ordering equipment to counting money collected in cans. With patients, doctors and nurses being centre stage, it is easy to assume that the administrative side of the work is routine and ordinary. Yet there is the same buzz of activity here. There is a feeling that, if the nursing wing is the heart of the place, this is where the resources needed to supply the lifeblood are processed. The running of the business side of the Hospice is a fascinating story in itself.

The lifeblood of the Hospice is funds – the maintenance of a steady and reliable income year in and year out. It took five years to raise enough money to buy Challenger Lodge and there were some anxious moments on the way. Even so it is easy to be complacent and think the money comes in easily and without too much effort. Those at the sharp end of this activity know differently. Money does come in and people do give generously but the reality is that it has never been as easy as it might seem. It may be that this misguided notion stems from the idea that being a Christian organisation means God is on-side and He gets on with it. The Christians at the Hospice would certainly say they believe they have the Almighty rooting for them but that, having faith it would all happen, has not meant sitting back and waiting for divine intervention. It takes hard work, dedication and commitment on the part of the Hospice staff responsible for fund-raising, the volunteers and the clubs and groups who donate money. Without this hard work the Hospice would not be in business. The committed Christians point out that you can forget your faith if you are not prepared to work for what you believe in – "faith without works is dead". Since Day One the costs, which are now considerable in terms of salaries, services, supplies, equipment and maintenance, have had to be met. Nor does "Divine Guidance" mean that the Hospice runs on a wing and prayer. If anything, there is a greater emphasis on business efficiency, good organisation and management, meticulous record-keeping and careful budgeting. Responsibility in putting the money to the best possible use, submitting decisions to scrutiny and accountability go back to long before such terms had their present day significance and meaning.

Despite the sentimentality and myth that surround the Hospice, it is a business entity that exists in the real world. Like any other enterprise it has had to cope with the changing business environment of the nineteen eighties, growing competitiveness within the charity sector, the uncertainties of inflation, economic recession in the nineties and maintaining its position in the face of these changes. It has had to move with the times and adapt to new developments, yet without losing sight of the basic values and aims which lie at the heart of it – that of meeting the needs of patients.

The competitive business culture in the nineteen eighties and changing strategies have had particular implications for the Hospice. Consumerism has grown steadily and, with it, the realisation that survival means knowing the market and what the customer wants in the way of goods and services. Selling has become more aggressive and companies have started promoting themselves as well as their products. Lastly, business efficiency has become essential in both public and the private sectors in gaining and holding onto a leading position. The results of these developments have been that consumer research has mushroomed; advertising, promotional activities and sponsorship of all kinds have taken off; companies have started to use image-makers and marketing companies to devise corporate identities and logos; and the silicon chip has revolutionised business practices. Some of these changes have been easy for the Hospice to embrace and in some it has been at the forefront – setting an example to the business community itself. Others have proved more controversial.

PUTTING PATIENTS FIRST

"Consumerism in action" is how St Columba's has been described and, since putting "consumers" or patients and their families first has always been the priority for the Hospice, in this respect St Columba's has taken a lead and set an example. The Hospice came into being largely because consumers were dissatisfied with the quality of care they were getting elsewhere. The Hospice's aim was to respond to this need for good care for terminally ill patients. From the outset, the provision of care was patient-centred – the staff and the procedures were there for the patient. Yet, for any organisation that starts off on a good footing, there is the danger of people becoming complacent. Unless efforts are made to guard against it, systems have a tendency to take over and become more important than those for whom they are provided. This is as true for the Hospice as any business entity. There are those who know that a pat on the back for the good work is important but also that resting on one's laurels will not maintain the Hospice's high standing. To counter complacency and keep everyone on their toes, staff at the Hospice have had to be their own critics. Since the early days, opinion polls and surveys have been carried out among GPs, community nurses, Hospice staff, patients and relatives and have provided much information on which to base different ways of doing things. This kind of constant scrutiny and feedback has been accepted as a way of staying ahead and allowing the Hospice to grow and flourish. But finding out what people want and how their needs might best be met is not always easy. Even in a hospice setting, patients are vulnerable consumers – dependent on others for their most basic needs. In an environment where so much is already done for them, it may be difficult to ask for something more or different. It is also easy to forget that the patients and families of today are not those of fourteen years ago and may have different needs. Finding ways of being objective, asking the right questions and allowing people to say honestly what they think and feel, is important in maintaining this patient-centred approach to care.

ADVERTISING AND THE CORPORATE IMAGE

Selling the service has been a different matter and new and innovative ideas in the eighties have caused concern. Radio and television appeals have always been successful but the idea of going into high profile selling of St Columba's has been met with mixed reactions. Some felt there were sound economic reasons for advertising, not least the fact that there were, and still are, many good causes competing for funds within Edinburgh and Scotland generally. Nationally, major telethon appeals such as Children in Need drew unprecedented sums. The NHS itself went into fund-raising on a massive scale – for example Edinburgh's Sick Children's Hospital Appeal. Internationally, we became aware of starving people in Africa through Live Aid and its aftermath. Many saw direct advertising as perfectly acceptable and voiced strong arguments in favour of using whatever methods were appropriate to raise money. Views such as, "What we do here provides a valuable service, we really have to tell people", and, "If you're in business, you're in a competitive situation", were voiced. Others saw advertising as the modern way of "spreading the gospel".

The views of those in advertising inevitably strengthened the case. One executive pointed to the need to educate the public who knew little about the work of the Hospice. "Edinburgh people give because they think it is a good cause, although they don't really know what it's about. They see it as a very worthwhile and religious-backed organisation that makes dying peaceful and helps people rediscover themselves before they die. They don't realise that, in fact, it's a very good hospital." Another factor in favour of advertising was the corporate identity. Most organisations spend money to create an image among the public. The Hospice needed to destroy the illusion and mystique, which did little to promote an understanding of it, and to promote the reality.

Others were reluctant to go down the advertising route. There was an uneasiness and a feeling that it was somehow distasteful – perhaps a fear that using modern business practices, such as advertising and marketing, would somehow taint the Hospice with a worldliness which was inappropriate. Marketing and advertising agencies seemed very remote from terminal illness. To some, it was as if bringing the Hospice and the agents of big business side by side was like getting God and Mammon together. Nor was it difficult to understand the apprehension. Advertising has often been seen to exploit the need for glamour and excitement in life and to sell images that can be misleading. The business of St Columba's, on the other hand, is about acceptance of truth. But within any sphere of activity there is good practice and bad practice and the same is true of advertising. There is advertising that does much to educate and inform the public and the industry itself has a wealth of professionalism, talent and creativity. The advertisers were keen to get involved. They saw that the Hospice had an image which did not do it justice. By setting the record straight and telling the public what went on behind the walls of St Columba's, they would broaden the appeal to many more people.

There were also issues that many felt could only be clarified through the media. It was difficult, in the late eighties, to assess how proposed changes in government support would affect the Hospice. In addition to grants from Lothian Health Board for eight beds and Fife Health Board for one bed, from April 1990 the Hospice would receive a 'top-up' sum to meet fifty per cent of running costs. The support was to be for all expenses for in-patient care, home and day care, education and administration but not the cost of running the appeal effort or capital and depreciation costs. This commitment was to run only until 1992. What would happen when the Health Service went into the contract situation in line with the White Paper was not clear. There was a feeling that such fifty per cent funding could work two ways. It might encourage people to give or it might lead them to sit back and think the Hospice was now secure, not realising that it still needed over £1,500,000 each year to keep the doors open with approximately £750,000 of this to be raised from voluntary sources. The Hospice was still very dependent on the goodwill of supporters.

The arguments about how to promote the Hospice were batted back and forth. Finally a decision was taken to move into direct advertising in the press, as long as it was done with care and sensitivity. The initial approach was low key. The first advertisement carried a lot of copy and the slogan "Miss a meal and say thanks" to point out to the public that many small sums add up to the cost of major repairs. The idea was to encourage giving by those who think small sums are of little value to a charity because they are mere 'drops in the ocean'. In this instance the major repair was the refurbishment of the nursing wing which required a sum of £100,000. The advertisement suggested if every reader was to contribute the cost of their next family meal, as a way of saying "thank you" that he or she did not require St Columba's services, then the building cares would be over.

Information was also the key in the press advertisement that ran in 1989. The headline "Charity can begin at home" was used to tell readers about the value and importance of the Home Care Service and to appeal for funds for the service.

The appointment of John Major as Chancellor of the Exchequer and the government's commitment to match voluntary donations 'penny for penny' presented an opportunity to tell the public "Every time you give to St Columba's, we get a Major contribution" and "Every time you dig in the Chancellor forks out". In this instance, a coupon was included as part of the advertisement to actively generate a response. The approach was successful. It caught the reader's eye, gave information about government funding and there was a good response.

Early in 1990 the Hospice tried a very different style of advertisement. A photograph with the disturbing caption "Please help this man to die", designed to draw the reader to the small print, appeared in the press. The copy continued, "Without fear, pain or sadness. With dignity, among friends. That's how Joe wants to die". Asking for funds for buildings, explaining government funding and even describing the work of the Home Care Service have been relatively easy to do through advertising. Presenting a more personal face of death as in "Please help this man to die" proved more difficult and controversial. It confronted the issue of dying. The photograph was that of a middle-aged man – somebody's husband and father – not an elderly person at the end of their life. Many people simply did not like it. They thought that it was in poor taste, offensive and insensitive. There were complaints and letters objecting to its direct approach to death. Despite the resistance, however, it proved successful both in terms of fund-raising for the Hospice and as a piece of creative advertising. In the Autumn of 1990, it won the Scottish Advertising Award for the best Direct Response Advertisement.

Derek Doyle's view is that advertising is not simply a matter of selling the services of the Hospice. Because he believes firmly that the Hospice will be evaluated in terms of how it changes attitudes to patients and people, he sees advertising as playing an important role in informing public opinion. He sees it as a challenge:

"I think they have a difficult job. If you think about the

Shirley Sibbald and Mary Young holding the awards presented to the
Hospice as "Scottish Computer User of the Year", 1989.
(Photo courtesy of The Evening News, Edinburgh)

Sheana Monteath and Katy Cooper receiving the keys for the new
Hospice shops van, 1990.
(Photo courtesy of The Evening News, Edinburgh)

Home Care Service, that's been going for thirteen years but if you ask a person in Edinburgh what they know about the Hospice, they talk about the building and care in the building. It's a selective thing and getting information across is tricky. This isn't just a product we are selling. It's much more than that. It's telling people what we are doing".

Early in 1991, the Hospice tried a new advertising medium. A short cinema commercial featuring the slogan "Help the dying live a little, give a little" was screened. Appearing in the middle of the usual selection of cinema advertisements, it had impact – there was silence, people were jolted and caught their breath. It tried very simply to encapsulate the Hospice philosophy, to get people to think and give. Other ideas are still to take shape. Finding sensitive and compassionate ways of communicating about death to the public may have its pitfalls. Death is the last of our taboos and the fact of the matter is that, however sensitively it is handled, there will be those who simply find it unacceptable and unpalatable. It will take time and patience to change attitudes.

SILICON CHIPS AND "NURSING THE FUNDS"

When St Columba's began in the late seventies, there was a feeling amongst the staff then that they were out on their own in Scotland. Being too far from St Christopher's in London and St Luke's in Sheffield to get help and support, everything had to be done from scratch. Systems had to be developed to encompass the very rapid growth of the Hospice and to keep everything working smoothly. A payroll of five very quickly grew to fifty. With the boom in the computer industry happening at this time, this was the obvious way to tackle the problems presented by growth. Having a senior banker on the executive committee, who understood the various applications to which computers could be put, helped to get this development off the ground.

Shirley Sibbald, who had been the Finance Officer since 1977, was given the responsibility for setting up what is now a very sophisticated computer system. It has not only streamlined administration but also has had a major input on the care side. None of the staff had experience of computers or considered themselves computer-literate. Shirley Sibbald recalled their reactions:

"I can remember the fears, the frights, the terror that we all experienced, but we had to get on and do it because we could not contain the development. Now it has become so efficient that people have time to think occasionally. At one time it was a pell-mell battle against time".

The staff at the Hospice describe themselves as being good at identifying the need and use to which to put computers and then going out and finding the programme or someone to write the programme for them. Accounts and a donor database were the obvious first applications. These were followed by the palliative care database. The collection of medical statistics was set up in 1986 and provides a retrospective look at patient care. It covers diagnosis, primary sites of carcinomas and symptoms of patients on admission. It also records treatment during the period, the outcome and where the patient died. The database is used mainly for research and teaching purposes.

Computerisation has contributed to the smooth running of the Hospice in a host of other ways. Equipment registers, staff lists, budgeting, and a volunteer database produce information at the touch of a button. Printed matter, such as newsletters, leaflets and annual reports, are produced in-house resulting in considerable savings.

Good management, commitment to efficiency and computerisation are in some ways more in keeping with a business at the leading edge of industry or commerce. When the Hospice won the 'Scottish Computer User of the Year' award in 1989, it certainly demonstrated that it is up there with the best of them. Since the bottom line here is not profit, the sixty four thousand dollar question is, 'How does all of this help Mrs Brown in the bed in the ward?'. Shirley Sibbald spells this out very simply:

"The efficient business management helps Mrs Brown stay where she is. If she had come in with a very rare carcinoma, the doctors would say, 'We had that lady, Mrs So-and-So, does anyone remember her name?'. Now you can go to the computer and ask it for details of patients who had this type of carcinoma over the last five years. You can then identify that patient, get the reference number, get out the file and see what you did for that patient".

It is all a far cry from the days of the half-penny fund, collecting cans, notes in shoe-boxes and the family atmosphere of the Hospice before the new nursing wing was built. How does the Hospice make sure that, in all this progress, the system does not lose sight of patients and the basic aim to give care?

The key to this is no different to managing the nursing side. It is by appointing staff who are both well qualified and personally motivated and who understand the work. Consequently, when a candidate for a post approached the Hospice with the attitude "It's not so much what I can do for you, it's what you can do for me" he was very politely told, "forget it!".

Having separate staff to handle money matters is important to patients. Over the years the nurses have found that patients do not like to talk to them about money. They prefer to discuss financial matters with the 'money lady'. A relative or patient may want help with benefits. Worries about financial problems come high up on the list for patients – second to the physical symptoms of pain and sickness. The stories of how these problems are dealt with reveal that administrative staff give the same caring and support to help relieve patients and relatives of financial worries as nurses and doctors give to help relieve pain. Support and advice are given in the same way – to help people stay in control of their lives:

"We had one lady who was divorced with three teenage children. She was worried there wasn't enough money to bury her. We persuaded her that she was going to be here a few weeks and she could save up her pension. She very carefully did that until she got to the stage where she knew there was enough money. Then she died. She was such a caring mother – this determination that her girls were not going to get into debt."

The administrative staff understand that what they do is as essential as the care of the patients – "managing the funds so that the care will always be there". The daily contact with relatives and patients also makes sure that they do not get cut off from the purpose of the Hospice. Shirley Sibbald explains how she kept in touch over the years and the support and encouragement she got from one patient in particular:

"I have been involved quite a lot on the patient side because I have handled patients' money, benefits, advised them, dealt with wills...all sorts of things over the years. I go and sit and talk with patients and relatives. We go and meet the relatives when they come in afterwards.

One patient I particularly remember. She was the most charming lady and she used to lie in bed in the most beautiful heather-coloured mohair blanket – her personal blanket. We had many difficulties over the years, many frustrations, lots of unhappiness. I was feeling particularly down one day and I had to go in and see her. She took my hand and said, 'Och, you're feeling a bit upset', and I said, 'Yes, it's got me under the skin'. She said, 'I've talked to you several times and I just have this feeling that you're the right person in the right job at the right time'. I can't tell you what that did for me. You bring out these things – they come back to you. And I walked out of her room and I thought, 'I must hang on to that through all the difficulties'. Life wasn't always easy after that, but I hung on to that – that I was meant to be here and that I had skills to be used.

We have relatives coming back – sometimes on a pretext – to bring a donation and they really want to talk. Over the years we have been able to pick up real cries for help and we put people in touch with one of the care staff or CRUSE. We get people coming in who are really under stress. So through all our professionalism and the business side we still have the contact. In a way I think this is the motivation that we get – it reminds us what it's all about and keeps our feet on the ground."

It is this down-to-earth but nevertheless caring approach to living and dying which makes the business ethic work alongside the Christian ethic. No-one is allowed to lose sight of why the Hospice is there, the purpose of advertising campaigns or computer systems. It shows very clearly that there need be no conflict between holding onto ideals and moving with the times. As long as patients and families needs remain central and changes are introduced for their benefit, the Hospice stays firmly rooted.

INTO THE FUTURE

"The most important thing the Hospice has done is that it has made people appreciate that they have got to take dying and terminal illness seriously. We may send patients to the Hospice or ask ourselves if we are doing as well as we can – and many departments are now doing a good job of looking after terminally ill patients. I see more and more large hospitals developing hospice-type facilities within the hospital as a result of seeing the good things that leading hospices, like St Columba's, do. We've been moving towards saying, 'that's the example, shouldn't we be looking to turning a corner of the hospital over to terminal care?'" These words, spoken by a hospital consultant, sum up what many in the medical profession see as the contribution of the Hospice. They indicate that involving medical colleagues outwith the Hospice and teaching has been mutually beneficial and that the Hospice is on the road to achieving the success for which Derek Doyle aims when he says, "What will matter in 2050 is not how many patients have been treated but the number of doctors and nurses, around Scotland and the world, who enjoy being honest with people. They can sit with the dying. They don't list them as disasters but they haven't lost one bit of their scientific security".

The reality, however, is that we are a long way from the ideal of having Hospice units integrated into hospitals. Hospice care is a luxury available only to a very small minority. There are many in the medical profession who admit there is a lot of poor terminal care and, by and large, a busy medical or acute surgical ward is not a good place to die. If a patient there has a condition regarded as inoperable and incurable, then there is still a high risk that his or her needs will not be properly met. There is still a great deal to be done but the achievements of the first fourteen years of the Hospice provide grounds for optimism. Doctors, nurses and many others have learned the importance of hospice care itself – something far more important than St Columba's.

The Hospice is not only there for the professionals, it sets an example for everyone. What good does it do if doctors and nurses see the value of the Hospice way of caring unless we can all share in it? The sharing grief, the sharing strength, the sharing ourselves is important for us all. Fred Benton is as aware as Derek Doyle that there has been a tendency for their work to back-fire on them, as the public has come to regard them as the "experts" – the only people who can do this work well:

"By providing care for the dying in this idyllic setting, are we encouraging people to say, 'We can't do it right ourselves, so Dad must come into the Hospice'? Someone hears about the Hospice and then there's pressure on the GP – as if the Hospice is the only place where people can die properly."

The Hospice does not claim sole rights to the care of the dying. St Columba's is there to show us all what can be done and not, as so many of us would like to think, to provide us with an excuse to stand back and say, "You get on with it, you can do it so much better". Derek Doyle and others have been honoured for the pioneering work they have done. Like all the doctors and nurses he is professional and caring, but he is no silver-haired guru. To put him or any of the staff on a pedestal and leave all the caring to them is no less than putting our own compassion somewhere out of reach and, in doing this, we deprive ourselves and others.

The Hospice is not something entombed or enshrined in Challenger Lodge – it is a way of life for the dying and those caring for them. The challenge for the 1990s is, through education and good public relations, to make that way of life more widely available. Another measure of the success of the Hospice in the future will be the extent to which all of us can care for the dying – sit with them, asking for practical support and help when needed, but not surrendering our loved ones and our compassion completely.

****

The story of St Columba's is very simple – that the Christian or caring ethic can and does work in the real world. The Hospice is not some remote and cloistered place of religious activity. It is about ordinary people who try to do a job well. It is a place where patients can be themselves, safe in the knowledge that they will be accepted for who they are and that their needs will be met. It is, in fact, very ordinary but difficult to accept or value as such, which is perhaps why people like to put a gloss of mystique over it.

The underlying message is that caring is a basic human value common to us all. The role of the Hospice in modern times is to remind us that any act of caring enriches the life of the person giving and the life of the person receiving – a basic truth that is all too often overlooked in our materialistic world. Giving of ourselves, in whatever small way, allows the core of ourselves, the spirit, to grow and we add something to the common good. The other side of St Columba's teaches that in giving we open ourselves to be given to. The dying give to the living in many ways – in telling others what happens at the end of life, that dying may hurt the body but it frees the spirit and that loved ones do live on in our memories and in our hearts. They give by telling us what is important in life. It is summed up by the patient who detected a discomfort and unease in a young nurse. "Don't try to be something that you're not, just be yourself", was her advice. She knew the value of what she was saying. When people feel "safe", as they so often say they do at St Columba's, they can drop their masks and protective armour. People who have carried great burdens of guilt or anger throughout their lives are finally able to forgive and make their peace with those they love. They let go the things that prevented them from being themselves. In doing so they often realise that, if they had done this years ago, their lives might have been different.

As for death itself, in the end ordinary men and women find they have the courage to face up to and go through the process of dying. It is an enormous waste that so many go through life fearful and afraid, without knowing that they have this courage all the time. These are enormously important lessons the dying teach the rest of us – what freedom we gain by letting go life's hurts and what courage we all have if we did but know it. If we are prepared to learn these lessons, they can free us to live our lives as they are meant to be lived.

There is still a long way to go in changing public opinion about death and dying and the Hospice has a part to play – whether by individuals talking about their experiences, through conferences or through the media. Yet there are signs that things are changing. The young have the most to lose by hiding from the truth and the most to gain of simply being themselves. Many are beginning to realise this and there is an openness and honesty among them and a willingness to talk and challenge. During the early days of the Gulf war a young British pilot was interviewed after returning from his first bombing raid over Baghdad. In the euphoria and excitement he confessed his fear, "You're afraid of

enemy flak, you're afraid of dying...you're afraid of everything".
That he spoke so openly of his fear and used the "D" word was
new. While the war itself was being beamed across nations by
satellite and cable TV, formal military language such as KIA
(Killed in Action), MIA (Missing in Action), "Take One Out",
"casualties", were used. These no doubt served to avert people
from dwelling on the reality of war and the unutterable grief
deaths caused. For the airman to be so honest and drop the mask
of the macho soldier – to let himself be seen simply as a vulnerable
young man, took courage. He spoke so obviously from the heart
there was no doubting that he spoke the truth. He was not alone
– there were many more who spoke openly of their fears.

In his novel "The Possessed" one of Dostoevsky's
characters says that the only reason man is unhappy is because
he does not know he is happy. Perhaps the same can be said of
courage – the only reason we are afraid of death and life is
because we do not know we have courage. If courage comes from
facing up to death then the story of St Columba's teaches a truth
that is important for young and old, for those in good health as
well as the terminally ill – that death is indeed a part of life and
recognising it as such can free us all to really live life to the full.

Appendix A

OFFICE BEARERS AND MEMBERS OF THE BOARD—1991

PRESIDENT
The Countess of Rosebery

VICE-PRESIDENTS
Miss A E Weatherill RGN SCM
T D S Bell TD SSC DL
A M Drysdale TD LLB JP

BOARD OF GOVERNORS
Chairman—The Hon. Lord Grieve VRD
Hon. Secretary—R J B Simpson MBE TD WS
Hon. Treasurer and Chairman Executive Committee—
    A D Monteath OBE TD CA
G B Archer
Colonel M B H Ashmore CBE
G M Burnside WS
John Bruce
Mrs Joan Cooper MBE
Professor R H Girdwood CBE MD PhD FRCPE FRSE
Sheriff W T Hook QC
The Rev Charles Robertson MA
Mrs B H Simpson
A F Wilkie
Lieut. General Sir David Young KBE CB DFC

PAST GOVERNORS
T D S Bell TD SSC DL
The Hon. Lord Birsay KT CBE TD LLD (Chairman 1977-1981)
Sir John Croom TD BA FRCPE FRCP
Mrs B B Dale-Green MBE
A M Drysdale TD LLB JP
Maurice Heggie
Miss E I W Hobkirk CBE TD LLD
Lieut. Col. R W Smith
R W Spittal FFA
Mrs M G Strathdee SRN
Miss A E Weatherill RGN SCM

Appendix B

USEFUL ADDRESSES

BACUP
(BRITISH ASSOCIATION OF
CANCER UNITED PATIENTS)
121/123 Charterhouse Street
London EC1M 6AA
071 608 1661 (Free phoneline
outside London: 0800 181199)
An information service on all types
of cancer staffed by experienced
cancer nurses. Produces leaflets,
booklets and a newsletter.

BRISTOL CANCER HELP
CENTRE
Grove House
Cornwallis Grove
Bristol Avon BS8 4PG
0272 743216
Residential and day centre:
provides a complimentary
approach to cancer for the whole
person. These holistic therapies can
be used safely with orthodox
medical treatments. Resource
information for patients and a
seminar/training programme for
health care professionals.

CRUSE – BEREAVEMENT CARE
Cruse House
126 Sheen Road
Richmond
Surrey YW9 1UR
081 940 4818

18 South Trinity Road
Edinburgh EH5 3PN
031 551 1511
Offers help, support and
counselling for bereaved people.

CANCER RELIEF MACMILLAN
FUND
15/19 Britten Street
London SW3 3TZ
071 351 7811

9 Castle Terrace
Edinburgh EH1 2DP
031 229 3276
Provides funding to establish
projects for the care of cancer
patients. It also provides financial
support to families where this is
appropriate.

CANCERLINK
17 Brtannia Street
London WC1X 9JN
071 833 2451

9 Castle Terrace
Edinburgh EH1 2DP
031 228 5557
Information, support and referral
service for people with cancer,
carers and health professionals.
Information on cancer support
groups.

CARERS' NATIONAL
ASSOCIATION
29 Chilworth Mews
London W2 3RG
071 724 7776

11 Queen's Crescent
Glasgow G4 9AS
041 333 9495

COMPASSIONATE FRIENDS
6 Denmark Street
Bristol BS1 5DQ
02272 74691
Offers friendship and support to
grieving parents who have lost a
child at any age, under any
circumstances.

HELP THE HOSPICES
34-44 Britannia Street
London WC1X 9JG
071 278 5668

HOSPICE INFORMATION
SERVICE
St Christopher's Hospice
51 Lawrie Park Road
Sydenham
London SE26 6DZ
081 778 9252
Provides a link and support for
health care workers and members
of the public seeking information
on the work of the hospice
movement. Publications include
"Choices", listing details of courses
on terminal care and bereavement.

LISA SAINSBURY FOUNDATION
8-10 Crown Hill
Croydon
Surrey CRO lRY
081 686 8808

MARIE CURIE CANCER CARE
28 Belgrave Square
London SW1X 8QG
071 235 3325

21 Rutland Square
Edinburgh EH1 2AH
031 229 8332
Provides hospice and community
nursing services.

MOTOR NEURONE DISEASE
ASSOCIATION
PO Box 246
Northampton NN1 2PR
0604 250505/22269
Helpline for patients and carers:
0800 626262

NEW APPROACHES TO CANCER
5 Larksfield
Englefield Green
Surrey TW20 0RB
0784 433610
Promotes the benefits of holistic
and self-help methods of healing.
Cancer patients learn how they can
help themselves through diet,
relaxation and a positive mental
and emotional attitude. Network of
self-help groups and holistic
practitioners.

TAK TENT
G Block Western Infirmary
Glasgow G11 6NT
041 334 6699/357 4519
Information, emotional support
and counselling for cancer patients,
relatives and professional staff.

Appendix C

FURTHER READING

I Don't Know What To Say: How to help and support someone who is dying.
    Robert Buckman, Papermac, 1988.

On Death and Dying. Elisabeth Kubler-Ross, Tavistock Publications, 1970.

Living with Dying. David Carrol, McGraw Hill, 1985.

Tears and Smiles: The hospice handbook. Martin Lewis, O'Mara Books, 1989.

The Hospice Alternative: Living with dying. Margaret Manning, Souvenir
    Press, 1984.